CRITICAL AND
CONSTRUCTIVE ESSAYS

CRITICAL AND
CONSTRUCTIVE ESSAYS

BY MOST REV.
ARCHBISHOP RICHARD DOWNEY, D.D., Ph.D., LL.D.

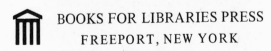
Essay Index Reprint Series

BOOKS FOR LIBRARIES PRESS
FREEPORT, NEW YORK

First Published 1934
Reprinted 1968

LIBRARY OF CONGRESS CATALOG CARD NUMBER:

68-8455

PRINTED IN THE UNITED STATES OF AMERICA

CONTENTS

CRITICAL AND CONSTRUCTIVE ESSAYS

WHERE DID THE WORLD COME FROM ?

(ADDRESS TO THE LIVERPOOL CATHOLIC UNIVERSITY SOCIETY)

THE term *God* connotes totally different ideas in different minds : to some it conveys the notion of a limited deity, a sort of younger god still in process of evolution ; to others it calls up the vision of an anthropomorphic being continually breathing vengeance, a blood-thirsty super-despot in the heavens ; to others again it conjures up the image of a glorified clergyman setting an impossibly high standard of conduct, and exacting unquestioning belief in incomprehensible theological formulæ ; whilst to many it brings the consoling idea of an all-loving Father ; and consequently, to ask the question ' is there a God ? ' is not a very satisfactory method of approaching the subject of theism. A more profitable method of approach is to begin, not with a somewhat elastic idea, but with a fact, the greatest fact known to us, the universe of which we ourselves are part.

I

Philosophy begins in wonder expressing itself in questionings. The desire to ask questions is very deeply rooted in the human breast. A little child can ask as many questions in five minutes as most of us cannot answer in five hours. Perhaps sometimes on a fine Sunday afternoon you have seen a little boy going for a walk with his father, and all the way along the little boy keeps saying : ' What's this, Father ? ' and ' what's that, Father ? ' And his father, if he is wise, says ' ask your mother.' He couldn't answer those questions, if his answers brought universal peace to the world to-morrow. For a child is very much of a philosopher. You have perhaps heard the story of the small boy who pointed to an animal in a field and said ' What's that ? ' His father answered ' that's a cow ' ; whereupon the child with acute penetration immediately asked ' why ? ' And answer there was none. Men and women are only children of a larger growth, and they, too, love to ask questions. The history of the human race on its intellectual side is the history of inquisitiveness, the history of the enquiry that man is everlastingly establishing into the nature and meaning of his surroundings. To-night I propose to direct your attention to the most fundamental of all these questions, to that which concerns itself with the interpretation of the universe. Now every rational being makes some interpretation of the universe ; each and every one of us has some theory as to its origin : the theory may be nebulous, it may even be fatuous, but we each have one. And it seems to me that all the various interpretations which have ever been offered may be classed under four headings :

(1) There is in the first place Pantheism which visualises all finite things in the universe as modes or appearances of one underlying fundamental nature, one ultimate reality sometimes regarded as mind, as in the Hegelian school, sometimes as matter, as in the materialistic scheme of Haeckel, and sometimes as a combination of mind and matter, as in the view of Spinoza, where matter and spirit are absolutely one without any real distinction. In any case the totality itself is envisaged as God, and we and everything in the universe as parts of the divinity, just as leaves are part of the tree. The most up-to-date form of Pantheism is the Bergsonian conception that God, somehow identified with nature, is blindly struggling to find Himself and fulfil Himself in much the same way that a tree struggles for growth. Pantheism is essentially monistic, unifying everything and explaining the many by the one.

(2) At the opposite pole we have pluralism, which makes no attempt at unification at all, but is content to explain the many by the many. It regards all finite minds in the universe as being themselves, in their very separateness, ultimate constituents of reality. It portrays the world as consisting of a vast number of spiritual units, variously called monads, subjects, souls or selves, of which the human soul is the highest known to us, but none of which is so high in grade as to be infinite or even supreme. We need not spend much time discussing the claims of pluralism, as it has failed to win many adherents because of its manifest defects ; for instance, in any pluralistic system, (1) each mind must obviously

produce its own universe unrolling it from within itself, and we are thrown into sheer solipsism. (2) Again pluralism offers no explanation whatever of the order which obviously connects the different minds, at least in their interchange of ideas, (3) and, finally, it gives us a universe with ragged edges and loosely knit parts like a blanc mange that has never been in a mould, unless it merges into monism, as indeed it generally does. William James in his work *A Pluralistic Universe*, clearly sees the hopelessness of the position, for he says ' May not you and I be confluent in a higher consciousness, and confluently active there, though we know it not ? ' This, surely, is tantamount to pleading for a monistic basis.

(3) As a third interpretation of the universe, we have agnosticism, which admits the necessity of some ultimate reality at the back of all phenomena, variously called the Absolute, the Unrelated, the Unconditioned, the Ideal, but which asserts that the human mind, being constituted as it is, cannot know anything of this ultimate reality beyond the bare fact of its existence. Agnosticism is an imposing and seductive word, carrying with it an air of deep learning and profound thought, and the man who calls himself an agnostic implicitly claims to be no common or garden fellow. Frequently, however, he knows nothing of any theory of knowledge or even that agnosticism is a theory of knowledge. Occasionally he knows even less than that, as is illustrated in the case of the dying man who refused to see any minister of religion, and when asked the reason said, ' I've lived an acrostic, and I'll die an

acrostic.' Huxley was wise when he selected the Greek word agnostic in preference to the Latin ignoramus. There is a good deal in a name.

As a matter of fact agnosticism is a theory of knowledge : it is defined as that theory of knowledge which ends in doubt, or disbelief of some or all of the powers of knowing possessed by the human mind. In a word, it is the opposite to gnosticism. Gnosticism attributed to the human mind a greater power of knowing than it actually possessed. Agnosticism denies to the human mind a power of attaining knowledge which it does possess. It is important to remember that agnosticism, as such, is a theory about knowledge and not about religion. This fact is frequently overlooked and the probe of empiric test confined illegitimately to the sphere of religious knowledge. The best refutation of agnosticism is to give it its full implication, when it renders both science and philosophy impossible, just as much as religion. The agnostic who accepts only what is ' verifiable by experience ' will have a scant store of knowledge. No agnostic has any business to believe that the earth revolves on its axis, or that the earth goes round the sun, since he has never experienced either motion. He knows these truths only by a process of induction, precisely the same process by which we know the existence of God. Strictly speaking, agnosticism is not an interpretation of the universe at all, but a sophisticated re-statement of the question.

(4) Finally, as an interpretation of the universe

there is theism, which for our present purpose includes also deism, since the latter system admits the existence of God, though it denies His providence, conceiving Him as content to sit aloft and watch the world go round. Theism holds that the universe and everything in it owes its origin to an infinite personal being, distinctive from the universe, whom we call God.

To-night I propose to put before you the reasons for a theistic interpretation of the universe, reasons which incidentally refute Pantheism, Pluralism and Agnosticism.

Before doing so I must make some preliminary observations by way of removing possible misconceptions. It has been pointed out that we come to a knowledge of our heavenly Father in much the same way as we come to a knowledge of our earthly father. We know the latter through the manifestations of his mind in his external actions, that is to say, we refer certain manifestations of intelligence to their cause, and so come to know that cause intimately. So, too, from the study of nature we arrive at a knowledge of the existence and nature of its ultimate cause. It is a simple process of inference, and no more difficult than that by which we come to a knowledge of our earthly father. This process in the case of the existence of God has been set forth in complicated metaphysical arguments, but it is not necessary to understand these arguments to arrive at a sure knowledge of God's existence, any more than it is necessary to master elaborate medical treatises on vision and digestion, in order to see or digest our food. In the same way, a man may have an unshakeable knowledge of the existence of God without ever having heard of the arguments. It must be clearly borne in mind that these arguments for the existence of God fulfil much the same function as the proof of a sum in arithmetic. They check the validity of our reasoning and guarantee the answer at which we have already arrived. The various arguments for the existence of God have been classified in many different ways, but I think it best to adopt the very simple classification of Kant, who divided them into ontological and cosmological arguments.

The word ontological is derived from the Greek ὄν, ὄντος which means ' being.' It was held that there is nothing affirmable of any being except its essence, and that essence is given in its definition. Hence the ontological argument argues from the essence or definition of the thing, rather than from the thing itself. The starting point of the argument then is not things, but ideas. Hence it is called the *a priori* argument, since it starts from the prior idea of the thing, and not from the thing itself as it exists. We shall have more to say of this argument later. The word cosmological is from the Greek word κόσμος meaning order, and was applied by the ancients to the world in which order is so conspicuous. Any argument from the world as it exists, and not merely from the idea of it, comes under this heading, and is called an *a posteriori* argument, in that it proceeds from the posterior thing and not from its prior concept. This cosmological argument may be stated in a variety of forms. St. Thomas Aquinas in the Summa, in the

III Article on the Existence of God, states it in five ways, arguing from the

1. motion
2. efficient causes
3. changeable character of things
4. degrees of perfection
5. order or design

which we perceive all around us. It is important to realise that they are not meant to be five different conclusive ways of proving the existence of an infinite personal being. Taken collectively, they are unanswerable. It is not contended that each one is self-sufficient, so that in considering them individually the scope of each argument must be borne in mind.

1. The complete argument underlying the five ways is based on the principle of causality, on the self-evident principle that every event requires a sufficient cause. A moment's reflection makes it obvious that this principle is as self-evident as the statement that the whole is greater than the part. Care must be taken to state it correctly. It is wrong, for instance, to say that everything that exists must have a cause. That is obviously going beyond the available evidence. The statement that every effect requires a cause is mere tautology. Stated as I have stated it, the principle cannot be denied. And as a matter of fact it never has been denied. It is sometimes said that Hume denied it ; but he did not. He instituted an enquiry as to why every event necessarily requires a cause. It was the necessity he was investigating. And he came to the conclusion

that the necessity is not intrinsic, but extrinsic. In his own elegant language, it is the ' offspring of experience engendered upon custom,' that is to say, we think it necessary because we have always found it so. The argument may be stated in popular form as follows :

Every human being is at some time faced with the problem of his own existence. The child asks itself ' where did I come from ? ' Soon it realises that it came from its parents, that they came from their parents, and so on, till it reaches the first pair, Adam and Eve, and is told that they were created by God. This is an intelligible answer and rests the child's mind.

But nowadays, in certain circles, the child is told that Adàm and Eve evolved from lower animal forms, back and back to the protoplasm. At once the child wants to know where that came from, and is informed that it developed in the course of æons of ages from azotoprotoplasm. That word ought to keep any child quiet, and yet it does not. The child persists in wanting to know where *that* came from. And well it might. The more mature mind, even, is confronted with the problem of this long chain stretching from the child to the azotoprotoplasm. No link in the chain is self-sufficient, nor can it account causally for itself or for the chain. What, then, are we to say ? Did the chain cause itself ? Clearly it could not do so, for the simple reason that, to cause itself, it would have to exist, and to be caused, it would have to not exist. Since it is impossible for any entity to exist and not exist at the same time, we are forced back upon the alternative

B

that the chain and everything in it was brought into being by some cause outside the chain, itself uncaused and containing within itself the adequate reason of its own existence : this cause uncaused is what men call God.

The earliest Greek philosophers, some 600 years B.C., were entirely concerned with cosmology, and more particularly with the origin of the world. They looked outward upon the world instead of inward upon their own lives, and occupied themselves in a search for the primary substance of the universe from which all else was supposed to have evolved. They were intrigued with the crude problem of material causality. Thales thought that the primary substance was water, Anaximander gaseous matter, Anaximenes air, Heraclitus fire, and a modern rationalist has reverted to their primitive simplicity, thereby illustrating the theory of eternal recurrence, in proclaiming the primary substance to be ether, oblivious of the fact that ether is at best a mere working hypothesis for the scientist. This rationalist, however, declares that ether is eternal, failing to see that if it be eternal it is also infinite, and therefore in some sense a materialistic god, so that the propounder of this view lands himself in much the same position as the schoolboy who asserted that Homer was not written by Homer, but by another person of the same name. With a view to illustrating how everything in the universe, including human beings, evolved out of ether, our rationalist says that this happened in much the same way as the diamond came from carbon or the oak tree out of the acorn. These are excellent illustrations, and there is only one thing the matter with them : they do not illustrate. The evolutions in his illustrations are perfectly natural and well understood processes. Not so the supposed evolution of the universe, comprising mind as well as matter, from ether. If the rationalist would show us a diamond evolving out of an acorn, or an oak tree evolving out of carbon he would be giving us illustrations to the point. The whole idea of an impersonal deity, whether material or immaterial, runs counter to the principle of causality, which requires that every cause must contain the perfections of its effects : that which gives light must have light, that which gives heat must have heat, and that which gave personality must have it. The personality of God is inferred from the fact that we ourselves, His creatures, are persons. It is inconceivable that God could call into existence something greater and more perfect than Himself : it would be like water rising above its own level.

2. The argument from change and from contingent beings. This is the very core and essence of the argument from causality, and it may be presented succinctly as follows :

Everything in the visible world is subject to change. Therefore everything is contingent : nothing in the universe has, as it were, a grip upon existence : existence is not of its very nature. Since everything in the world is contingent, then everything may or may not exist, and consequently everything might be in mere objective potency to existence. But nothing can pass from potency to act except by receiving an impetus from something already in act. Hence the mere fact that there are contingent beings is in itself a conclusive proof that there must be a necessary being, a being that has a grip upon existence, a being whose very essence is existence. Hence the aphorism of the schools ; if there ever had been nothing there never could have been anything at all. Without the concept of a necessary being we should be in the position of the Indian who maintained that the world was supported by an elephant, the elephant by a tortoise, and the tortoise by nothing at all.

3. The teleological argument is in reality another part or phase of the cosmological argument, sometimes contemptuously styled Paleyism by people who have misconceived its character. It is popularly known as the argument from the order in the universe, and it is against this argument in particular that modern objections are chiefly lodged. Briefly we may state the argument thus : wherever order meets us, the natural, the necessary and inevitable inference is that it is the result of intelligence. But order meets us everywhere in the universe. It leaps up to the naked eye and stretches far beyond the disciplined vision assisted by all the instruments and appliances of science. Therefore the universe is the work of intelligence. A glance at the chief objections urged against the argument suffices to bring out its real force. (i) Hume, Kant and Mill in slightly different ways contended that the universe cannot be the work of an infinite God because it is a mark of imperfection to use means to an end, as God must have done in the work of creation. Obviously this is so only when it is of the essential

nature of the worker to act in this way, and it has never been maintained by theists that the Creator could not operate differently. It is merely the method which He *de facto* adopted, and it is a mark of perfection to do one's will and not the will of others.

(ii) It is frequently said that the argument from design is merely an argument from analogy, and that all arguments from analogy are fallacious. Now it is true that Socrates argued from the analogy that a statue requires a sculptor, and that 2000 years later, Paley argued from the analogy of a watch implying a watchmaker, but the force of the argument in both cases is that of inference, and the inference from the universe to a Creator is not more complicated or less legitimate than that from the statue to the sculptor or from the watch to the watchmaker. Though analogies have been used, the argument itself is not one of analogy simply, but of induction.

(iii) Darwin's objection to the argument from design is indeed a curious one. He did not accept it because, as he says, he could not find order everywhere in nature. He failed to realise that, if there were only one instance of design in the universe, it would be sufficient to prove the existence of an intelligent designer. It would not, of course, prove the designer infinite, but it is not claimed for this argument, taken separately, that it does more than prove an intelligent designer.

(iv) The favourite method of evading the force of the argument has always been to profess to account for the cosmos by describing the manner in which it has evolved. By a sort of legerdemain, description is substituted for explanation. It is as if we sought to show that a watch need not have had a maker, by giving a minute description of the way in which the hands are moved by the internal mechanism. Evolution, says a prominent rationalist, has made an end of Paleyism. W. G. Ward cleverly illustrates the fallacy of this kind of reasoning by supposing the case of a philosophical mouse imprisoned in a piano, instituting an enquiry into the cause of the music. The sound, it argues, results from the vibration of the strings ; the vibration is caused by the blows of the hammers ; 'and so much at least is evident now—viz., that the sounds proceed not from any external and arbitrary agency—from the intervention, e.g., of any higher will—but from the uniform operation of fixed laws.' (*Philosophy of Theism*, Vol. II, pp. 172, 173.) Rationalists, like the mouse, fail to realise that laws do not exist of themselves, but postulate an intelligent lawgiver.

(4) I want to say just a few words about the moral or *ethical argument*, as, according to some thinkers, it is the strongest of all. Kant, for instance, rejected all the metaphysical arguments : he contended that any argument from pure reason is bound to be fallacious. Only practical reason, according to Kant, could lead to any valid result. With Kant, 'I ought' occupied the same fundamental place in his philosophy as 'I think' did with Descartes. If you deny the ethical 'ought,' he contended, you cannot act in consonance with right, i.e. practical reason. There is a moral law imposed upon our being and this moral law implies a lawgiver. It is

what is popularly called the argument from conscience. We may ignore conscience, but we cannot dispute its existence : it sits in silent judgment on all our actions. Whence comes the voice of conscience ? Evolutionists have tried to explain it as the product of evolution, but it is certainly not that. Huxley realised this when he said : ' Ethical nature, if born of cosmic nature, is certainly at enmity with its parent.' (*Evolution and Ethics*). In the utilitarian interests of mankind it ought to have been evolved out of existence long ago. But here it is in all its primitive vigour. There is no way of explaining this ethical ' ought ' except as a law imposed upon our being by a lawgiver from without.

(5) *The Argument from Common Consent.* This argument is not infrequently misrepresented by opponents in their endeavours to refute it. It is stated by them as though its force lay precisely in the fact that all men, or at least the majority of mankind, believe in the existence of God, thereby embodying the fallacy that what the majority believe must be true. This is, of course, a grotesque caricature of the real argument which is a psychological one, based on the fact of universal belief in a special set of circumstances. The fact that all men, with a few sophisticated exceptions, believe in the existence of God is hardly in dispute. Testimonies ranging from Cicero and Plutarch to such modern ethnologists as Tylor, Max Müller, Ratzel, Quatrefages and Gerland can easily be cited. The psychological implication is that if, in the circumstances, the universal belief of mankind could be a mere

delusion, human reason would be essentially fallacious and incapable of ever attaining, with certainty,
to truth. The psychological aspect of the argument
from common consent was seen by the stoic philosophers who insisted that this universal belief springs
from a feeling innate in man : ' *omnibus innatum et
in animo quasi insculptum esse Deos.*' (De Nat.
Deor. II, 5.)

We must note particularly the circumstances of
this universal belief in the existence of God. The
belief does not depend on the inspection of things
outside oneself alone, but can be arrived at by
considering man's own nature ; and, furthermore, it
is not concerned with a purely academic matter, but
with one of great practical importance. This conviction is not, as frequently claimed, on all fours
with the one-time universal belief in the sun's going
round the earth. The latter belief was based solely
on observation of external phenomena, and could
not be checked by comparison with the phenomena
of man's inner life. Moreover, it made no difference
to man's life whether the sun went round the earth
or vice versa. It was not a question vitally affecting
him—he had no practical interest in its solution.
But the question of God's existence does vitally
affect him—there is no man who does not want to
know, no man who does not strive to know, the
answer. It is in fact *the* question of questions, upon
his attitude to which the whole tenor of a man's life
depends. The objection that both civilised and
savage nations believed not in one God, but in many
gods, does not militate against the argument for a
Creator. Emerson forestalls the same objection

urged against the diversities of beliefs concerning immortality : ' I know well,' he says, ' that where this belief once existed it would necessarily take a base form for the savage and a pure form for the wise ;—so that I only look on the counterfeit as a proof that the genuine faith has been there.' (*Letters and Social Aims*, Emerson's Works, Vol. VIII, Riverside Edition, p. 308.)

We must now consider the famous ontological argument to which we have previously alluded. It is so subtle that it could have been put forward only in an age which had reached an advanced stage in metaphysical speculation, and consequently it is entirely unknown before the eleventh century. It was first propounded by St. Anselm (A.D. 1033–1109) and its inspiring motive was to start on common ground with the atheist, namely, with the mere conception of God. St. Anselm enunciated his argument thus : ' This good, which is such that it is impossible to conceive any greater, cannot exist in the mind only ; for were it so, it would be possible to conceive a good that was yet greater, namely, one which would exist not only in the mind, but in reality. If we can conceive a good which we are unable to conceive as being without existence, this good would be greater than one we are able to conceive as being without existence, therefore the latter, contrary to our definition, would not be the greatest good conceivable.' (*Proslogium*, Ch. II.)

In syllogistic form the argument runs :

God is a being greater than whom nothing can be conceived.

But a being that exists outside the mind as well

as in it as an idea, is greater than a being which exists merely as an idea.

Therefore God exists outside the mind as a reality and not merely in it as an idea.

This argument gave rise to a great deal of controversy as to its validity.   It was championed by St. Bonaventure and Henry of Ghent, and revived in various forms by Descartes and a number of thinkers in the eighteenth century.   In St. Anselm's own day it was assailed by Gaunilo in a work which contains the germ of all the criticism made in modern times by Gassendi and Kant.   It must be admitted that much of the criticism is beside the mark. Gaunilo, and later Kant, tried to expose the fallacy of the argument by parodying it, the former by applying what he conceived to be the argument to a lost island, and the latter to a hundred dollars. Gaunilo's effort was as follows :

I can conceive the most perfect of all possible islands, lost to all the world.

But an island that exists in reality is more perfect than one that exists only as an idea.

Therefore there exists in reality the most perfect of all possible islands, lost to all the world.

To this St. Anselm replied that if Gaunilo *could* conceive the idea of the most perfect of all possible islands, he, St. Anselm, would find that island for him and see that he never lost it again.   The precise point of St. Anselm's argument is that God, and only God, is a being greater than whom nothing can be conceived.   The argument, from its very nature, cannot be applied to anything but God, and all the entertaining parodies leave it untouched.   It was rejected by the Schoolmen generally, and by St. Thomas Aquinas in particular, on quite another ground, namely, that it makes an illegitimate transition from the order of thought to the order of reality. Following St. Thomas we do not base our proof of the existence of God on any ideas but on things as they are, the universe as it is, the world as we know it. The more we know of nature the more clearly do we see that it postulates an Infinite Personal God.

Centuries ago, Bacon pointed out that, whilst a slight taste of philosophy may dispose the mind to indifference to religion, deeper draughts bring it back to God.

RATIONALISING THE GODS

(From the 'Clergy Review,' January, 1931)

IN these days when speculative theology is largely neglected outside the Catholic Church, when metaphysics are at a discount and the inner light of experience has proved to be a will-o'-the-wisp, we are bidden by the Enlightened to betake ourselves to the study of comparative religion as to the only sure way to the understanding of the genesis and significance of all spiritual phenomena. The rationalist anthropologist, especially if he has dabbled in psycho-analysis, is ready to demonstrate how man with his rationalisations and sublimations, his introversions and extroversions, his phobias and libidos, in the course of the proliferating ages, has evolved out of his own inner consciousness and in his own image a god, whereas, in the memorable and tremendous words of Betsey Prig, 'there's no sich a person.'

The methods employed to produce this result are as fascinating as they are fallacious, and the celerity and ingenuity with which new anthropological theories are substituted for old ones, before your very eyes, so to speak, might well excite the envy of the expert conjurer. These theories, new and old, separately and mixed, filter down to the masses in

the picturesque inaccuracies of the ' scientific '
popularisers who dispense culture in monthly parts,
or in *Outlines*, or in chatty little articles in the
Sunday Press. The result is that nearly everybody
gets a tinge of rationalism in his light literature.

A good start is a great help in a race, and it must
not be forgotten that for a long time rationalists had
practically a monopoly in the study of comparative
religion. They proclaimed it a science, laid down
its principles, and explained away the belief in the
existence of God entirely to their own satisfaction.
It will be some time yet before fact catches up to
fiction.

Nowadays it is amongst the cultured classes that
rationalists search for living witnesses to disbelief,
but in the old days they claimed spiritual kinship
with the primitive savages. For with the aid of the
new science, had they not discovered whole tribes of
aboriginals who had no religion and knew no God—
natural born agnostics ? Clearly then, primitive
man had no religion, and God was invented thousands of years later by cunning priests for their own
advantage. This theory gained favour rapidly because it fitted in so beautifully with the general
evolutionary principle, that is to say, with the
particular general evolutionary principle which was
accepted in those days. There were difficulties, of
course. Why, for instance, there were priests before
there were gods, and what precisely priests did before
there was any religion, were amongst the problems
which clamoured in vain for elucidation. But time
is a great solver of problems. With the passing of
the years the godless tribes also passed, and kept on

passing till they passed out of existence, thereby solving the riddle of the anomalous priests.

But the godless tribes certainly had their day. Time was when the Andaman Islanders were a great consolation to the leaders of rationalist thought. Reams upon reams were written about the ' godless Andamanese,' and more would have been written, had not an educated Englishman, who had lived amongst the islanders for eleven years and really understood their language, put an end to the nonsense by testifying that the Andamanese not only had a religion, but a profoundly philosophical religion with a distressingly elaborate mythology.[1] Frankly, the Andamanese were a disappointment, but they were soon succeeded as exhibits by the Australian Blacks, with no less a person than Huxley as sponsor for their agnosticism. On what precise grounds we know not, but he stoutly declared that amongst these natives ' no cult can properly be said to exist.' However, they fared no better than the Andamanese, and were speedily dismissed from the highbrow company to which, strictly speaking, they ought never to have been admitted. This came about through the influence of Howitt, a distinguished ethnologist who, unlike Huxley, had studied the Australian tribes at first hand. As an authority on these tribes he is second to none, and this is what he wrote : ' I venture to assert that it can no longer be maintained that the Australians have no belief which can be called religious, that is, in the sense of beliefs which govern tribal and individual morality under a supernatural

[1] *The Making of Religion*, by Andrew Lang, p. 194.

sanction.'[1] That was the end of the Australian Blacks as human documents of atheism.

Next came the Indians, all the way from Guiana, presented by Mr. Im Thurn as the original genuine congenital atheists who ' know no god.' As in the case of the Andamanese and the Australians, it turned out that the impiety of the Indians was much over-rated. It took some time to penetrate the *disciplina arcani* which prevented the Indians from manifesting their sacred mysteries to the prying eyes of the unsympathetic foreigner, but at long last it became clear that the natives of Guiana were as profoundly religious as the rest of primitive mankind, if not indeed more so since they boasted a Valhalla and an Olympus of their own, and worshipped the Supreme Spirit under the titles of ' Our Maker ' and ' Our Father.' There was no help for it, they were ignominiously dismissed from the ranks of rationalism. But the search for godless tribes went on, and goes on, despite the testimony of such eminent authorities as Max Müller, Ratzel, de Quatrefages, Tiele, Waitz, Gerland, and Peschel, all of whom are agreed that there are no races of men without religious belief and practice. Professor Tylor astutely remarks that the case of godless tribes is similar to that of the tribes who are said to exist without language or without fire, for, says the Professor, ' as a matter of fact the tribes are not found.'[2]

It was most annoying of these untutored savages to have gods, and something had to be done about it. Something was done. It was observed that

---

[1] *Journal of the Anthrop. Institute,* 1885.
[2] *Primitive Culture,* Vol. I, p. 368.

there was a great similarity, a remarkable family likeness, between the gods of different tribes. It was concluded, therefore, that the different tribes had borrowed from each other and ultimately from some common source. But what common source ? Surely from the prejudicial teaching of Christian missionaries and possibly also from the disciples of Islam, both of whom were held to have borrowed from the ancient mythologies.

This theory of loan-gods held the field for some considerable time. It was fascinating fun to identify Isis with Venus, and Venus with Ceres, and Ceres with Rhamnasia, and Rhamnasia with the Kaitish Atnatu. There were no rules, so anybody could play. However, impartial investigators pointed out that what was wanted was evidence, not of similarity amongst the gods, but of *borrowing* on the part of the tribes. Thus Professor Rhys Davids insisted that ' the comparative method will be of worse than no service if we imagine that likeness is any proof of direct relationship, that similarity of ideas in different countries shows that either one or the other was necessarily a borrower. . . . It would, of course, be going too far to deny that coincidences of belief are occasionally produced by actual contact of mind with mind ; but it is no more necessary to assume that they always are so, than to assume that chalk cliffs, if there be such, in China, are produced by chalk cliffs in the Downs of Suffolk. They have no connection one with another, except that both are the result of similar causes. Yet this manner of reasoning is constantly found, not only through the whole range of the literature of the subject from classical times downwards, but even in the works of the present day.'[1] So also the renowned M. Cumont writes : ' Resemblances do not necessarily imply imitation. Similarities of ideas or practices ought to be explained, without any reference to borrowing, by community of origin.'[2]

The evidence of missionaries was, of course, always suspect, though the missionaries abroad, unlike the rationalists at home, at least knew the language of the people about whom they gave evidence. Furthermore, these missionaries, as men of God, generally succeeded in winning the confidence of the natives amongst whom they laboured, and of learning from them the hidden things of the spiritual life which were never revealed to the profane. But quite apart from missionary evidence it was easily established that there were many tribes who had never fallen under the influence either of Christianity or of Islam, and yet had gods in abundance, and rites and ceremonies and all the appurtenances of religion.

What about these tribes ? Well, said the rationalists, after all they are poor polytheists without any real concept of God as the Creator and Father. And here again the rationalists were wrong for, oddly enough, even primitive savages sometimes display a lack of consistency in reasoning which would reflect credit on a modern higher education. Since the tribes were polytheists, logically they had no right to be monotheists, that is to say, they had no right

---

[1] *The Origin and Growth of Religion, as illustrated by some points in the history of Indian Buddhism*, pp. 3, 4.
[2] *Les Religions Orientales*, p. 13.

C

to acknowledge and worship one Supreme Omnipotent Being. Nevertheless they did. M. Albert Réville, the great authority on native Amerind religions, writing of the numerous gods of Mexico and Peru, says : ' Each one of these deities received in his turn epithets which seem to attribute omnipotence to him and to make him the sole creator.'[1] Nor is there anything in this peculiar to the religions of Mexico and Peru. ' This is the case,' continues Réville, ' in all polytheistic systems, whether in Greece, Persia, and India, or in Mexico and Peru. It only proves that where man worships, he never limits the homage he renders to the object of his adoration ; but if he is a polytheist he has no scruple in attributing the same omnipotence to each of his gods in turn. It is much the same with the worthy curés in our rural districts, whose sermons systematically exalt the saint of the day, whoever he may be, to the chief place in paradise.'[2] The one fact that emerges clear is that the natives of Mexico and Peru had a concept of an Omnipotent Creator, whom they sought to worship. It must not be forgotten that, as Dr. Jevons has pointed out, polytheism equally with monotheism, springs from the idea of God. ' And if monotheism displaces polytheism, it does so because it is found by experience to be the more faithful interpretation of that idea of God which even the polytheist has in his soul.'[3] The polytheist, notwithstanding the diversity of deities in his Pantheon, many of them, by the way, mere

[1] *Origin and Growth of Religion, as illustrated by the Native Religions of Mexico and Peru*, by Albert Réville, p. 248.
[2] *Ibid.*, p. 248.
[3] *The Idea of God in Early Religions*, by F. B. Jevons, p. 156.

culture-heroes, may yet believe in an All-Father, a Creative Being, whose origin stretches far away beyond the ken of man, into the realm of the everlasting.

It could be denied no longer that there were tribal gods which had not been borrowed, which were, in fact, as indigenous to the soil as the natives themselves. The urgent need now was for a plausible theory which would account for these gods on a purely rationalistic basis. Promptly ponderous papers were written on the evolution of the idea of God, it being taken for granted that even the savage's idea of God must have evolved from some terrestrial concept. Various evolutionary theories were put forward, the earlier ones for the most part resting on the hypothesis of animism.

We may define animism in the words of Mr. Lewis Spence as ' the bestowal of a soul (Lat. *anima*) upon all objects.'[1] It is supposed that the savage regards everything in the universe as being constructed on similar lines to himself, and consequently endowed with powers of thought, of speech, of passion, of love and hatred. He attributes the whole gamut of human emotions to the sun and to the moon, to the winds and to the waves, to the trees and to the flowers, to the rocks and to the caves, just as much as to the animals who serve or attack him ; for all the knowledge possessed by savages, says Gomme, ' is that based on their own material senses, and therefore when they apply that knowledge to subjects outside their own personality they deal with them in terms of their own personality.'[2] But

---

[1] *An Introduction to Mythology*, p. 17.
[2] *Folklore as an Historical Science*, p. 132.

in what rationalistic manner did the untutored savage come to realise that he himself had a soul of a spiritual character ?   According to Tylor the savage logically inferred it from ' two groups of biological problems present to the mind of man : (1) What is it makes the difference between a living body and a dead one, what causes waking, sleep, trance, disease and death ?   (2) What are these human shapes which appear in dreams and visions ? '[1]

Observe that the primitive savage is supposed to have attained to the abstract notion of spirit chiefly by way of introspection, and then, with a passion for uniformity, to have bestowed spirits on everything in nature.   Furthermore, it is pointed out, that there is a hierarchy amongst these spirits, and that consequently the savage has only to continue his thoughts on evolutionary lines to produce one Supreme Spirit, the great All-Father, the final figment of man's imagination.

Surely any impartial investigator must feel that the abstract reasoning involved in animism is beyond the intellectual powers of simple savages.   As Professor Jastrow says : ' Animism, as a theory of belief, assumes a quality of reasoning which transcends the horizon of primitive man.'[2]   As a matter of fact, animism is an attempt at a primitive philosophy, an effort to establish some kind of principle of causation.   It needs to be borne in mind that primitive savages do not so much attribute a spirit to everything as personify the things around them ;   and this they do as a rough and

[1] *Primitive Culture*, Vol. I, p. 428.
[2] *The Study of Religion*, by Morris Jastrow, p. 182.

ready solution to the cosmological problem which engaged the attention of the earliest Greek philosophers, the problem of change. Whereas the Greeks sought to know whether the ultimate reality was static or dynamic, the savage merely observed that everything in nature is fleeting, transient, with no grip upon existence, and almost as variable as himself. Instead of betaking himself to metaphysics like the Greeks, the savage set out to interpret the universe in an anthropomorphic way. But he worshipped God with barbaric dances long before he philosophised. He felt the need of propitiating the Power upon which all else depended long before he sought to explain the dependence. As Professor Jastrow points out : ' Religious manifestations, however, precede the appearance of animism as an explanation of the universe, and hence as a theory of the origin of religion, the latter would be defective.'[1]

But even supposing that animism could be shown to be anterior to all religious practice, it would not follow that animism had given rise to religious belief. There is not a shred of evidence for the so-called evolution of theism from animism ; on the contrary, there are the gravest possible objections to such a theory. ' If man was without religion before the animistic theory presented itself to the mind,' says Professor Jastrow, ' animism by itself would not have led to the rise of religion. The emotions excited by a strange-looking tree or stone could not have been of such a character as to have kindled the divine spark in man ; and however deep

[1] *Op. cit.*, p. 182.

the impression made by such phenomena, as storms and lightning, may have been, the mere personification of these powers would not have led to bring into play the religious feelings—hitherto dormant. . . . In seeking, therefore, for the origin of religion, we must look for something which could stir his emotions deeply and permanently ;   which could arouse thoughts that would henceforth never desert him and would prompt him to certain expressions of his emotions and thoughts, so definite and striking as to become part and parcel of family and tribal tradition.   Animism answers none of these conditions.   Even the ceremonial to which it gives rise— the propitiation of powerful spirits, or the exorcising of evil ones—would have no chance of becoming permanent institutions without a substratum of belief that passes beyond the bounds of animism itself.'[1]

Mr. H. G. Wells, in his *Outline of History*, after very properly remarking that it is not for him to embark on theological discussions, adds : ' But it is a part, a necessary and central part, of the history of man to describe the dawn and development of his religious ideas and their influence on his activities.'[2] Unfortunately, Mr. Wells at different times gives different descriptions of that dawn and development.   His description in the last edition of the *Outline* is decidedly different from that set forth in earlier editions, and perhaps the explanation is to be found in the Introduction to the definitive edition, where we read, ' Pamphlets against the *Outline* by

[1] *Op. cit.*, pp. 183, 184.
[2] Definitive Edition, p. 62.

Mr. Gomme and Dr. Downey and an article or so
by Mr. Hilaire Belloc have also been useful in this
later revision.'[1]

In his earlier editions Mr. Wells adopted what he
calls the ' Old Man ' theory as to the making of gods.
The theory is simplicity itself : the Old Man of the
tribe dies, he is venerated after his death, marvellous
tales are told of him, his fame grows in song and
story, till finally he is deified. *Sic fit conversio tota.*
In his earlier editions Mr. Wells referred his readers
to Grant Allen, as though that facile populariser
was an original source, for a scientific exposition of
the ' Old Man ' hypothesis. He does not do so in
his definitive edition possibly because it had been
pointed out to him that Grant Allen had merely
democratised Herbert Spencer and had done that so
badly as to be thrown over in the Rationalist Press
Association's manual on the non-existence of God.[2]
In his definitive edition Mr. Wells still clings to his
' Old Man ' hypothesis, but with a weakened faith,
since he has now heard of, and mentions Sir E. B.
Tylor's animistic theory as well as one or two more
recent speculations which appeal to Mr. Wells's
bright imagination as plausible factors in the evolution of gods. Clearly he has learnt something since
he first took to instructing the public on the origin
of religion. And this is well if only on the principle
that he who drives fat oxen should himself be fat.
Alas, his case may be taken as typical of that of
other popularisers, especially where anything religious is concerned. They acquire knowledge on

[1] P. 6.
[2] *Some Errors of H. G. Wells*, by Richard Downey, p. 10.

the instalment plan of learning whilst earning. In
the unlikely event of their running to a tenth edition,
they would be moderately well equipped to write
a first.

Of the theory which Mr. Wells had the temerity to
set before thousands of readers as accounting for the
origin of religion on a naturalistic basis, Professor
Jastrow, after dismissing Tylor's animistic theory,
says : ' Still less satisfactory is the theory chiefly
associated with Herbert Spencer, which traces religion back to the worship of ancestors under the
guise of ghosts as its sole factor. The theory rests
on the supposition that the deities worshipped by
primitive men are, in reality, the spirits of his
ancestors.'[1]

Now all the available evidence tends to show that
ancestor-worship is a luxury which appeals only to
comparatively sophisticated minds, to the cultured
Chinese, for example, or, in a lesser degree, to the
Japanese, the Egyptians and the Assyrians. In the
decadence of Rome emperors were deified, but no
such apotheosis obtained amongst really primitive
tribes. Savages extolled and glorified their departed
great men, but even these heroes were rigorously
excluded from the choice circle of the immortals. It
is utterly impossible for the idea of a deathless god
to have evolved, in the savage mind, out of the idea
of a dead ancestor. The Supreme Being of the
savage belonged to a world that knew no death, the
ghost of a dead man could not enter there. Ghosts
and gods were never confused by the savage mind,
however much they may be confused in the minds

---

[1] *The Study of Religion*, p. 184.

of rationalists. ' Ghosts,' says Crawford Howell Toy, ' are shadowy doubles of human beings, sometimes nameless, wandering about without definite purpose except to procure food for themselves, uncertain of temper, friendly or unfriendly according to caprice.' ' The god,' on the other hand, ' appears to have been at the outset a well-formed anthropomorphic being. His genesis is different from that of the ghost, spirit, ancestor, or totem. These, except the spirit, are all given by experience.'[1]

It is difficult to understand how anyone acquainted with the facts can dissent from the conclusion reached by Dr. Jevons : ' Religion did not originate from ancestor-worship, nor ancestor-worship from religion.'[2] ' Certain Greek families,' he tells us, ' believed that they were descended from Zeus, and they worshipped Zeus, not as ancestor, but as god. The " deified ancestor " theory, however, would have us believe that there was once a man named Zeus, who had a family, and his descendants thought that he was a god. . . . The fact is that ancestors known to be human were not worshipped as gods, and that ancestors worshipped as gods were not believed to have been human.'[3]

The ancestor-worship theory as to the origin of gods is chiefly interesting on account of the extravaganzas of Grant Allen, Huxley, and Spencer. Having agreed that the Jews ' invented ' monotheism, and then in some mysterious way, not explained, communicated it to all other nations, it was incumbent

---

[1] *Introduction to the History of Religion*, by Crawford Howell Toy, p. 266.
[2] *Introduction to the History of Religion*, by F. B. Jevons, p. 302.   [3] *Ibid.*, p. 197.

on the three wise men to produce some evidence of
ancestor-worship amongst the Jews. Nothing
daunted, Grant Allen stoutly declared that in
Jehovah Himself ' we may still discern the vague
but constant lineaments of an ancestral ghost-
deity,' and then, remembering something of the
Scriptures, he adds very truly, ' as in a glass
darkly ' ;[1] so darkly, in fact, that Huxley and
Spencer were constrained to institute a systematic
search of the Scriptures for satisfactory examples of
ancestor worship. Huxley, at his wits' end, appeals
first of all to ' the singular weight attached to the
veneration of parents in the Fourth Command-
ment,'[2] and then, on some esoteric theory of his
own, to the Ark of the Covenant which, in Huxley's
considered judgment, ' may have been a relic of
ancestor-worship.' However, as a distinguished
rationalist once remarked, may-be's are not honey-
bees, and Huxley's pronouncement about the Ark
is one of those things which his disciples are anxious
to forget. In the end the Father of Agnosticism
accuses some unscrupulous persons unknown of
having suppressed the evidences of ancestor-
worship throughout the Bible in the interests of
monotheism—presumably on the principle that the
end justifies the means. Herbert Spencer gracefully
retires from an equally fruitless search with the
comforting reflection that ' the silence of their (the
Jews') legends is but a negative fact, which may be
as misleading as negative facts usually are.' In
other words, the Synthetic Philosopher is prepared

[1] *The Evolution of the Idea of God*, p. 68.
[2] *Science and Hebrew Tradition*, p. 308.

to bolster up a theory which has not a shred of evidence in its support.

It would seem that Grant Allen, Huxley and Spencer are by no means unworthy successors of an earlier exponent of more or less the same theory, M. Leclerc, who solemnly propounded the view that Greek mythology consisted simply of the diaries of rugged old seafaring men of Ionia. Little did these sea-dogs think in their buccaneering days that in their ungodliness they were carving for themselves niches in the Pantheon. Rationalism generally is strong in affirmation, but weak in proof. No proof is offered that there ever has been any evolution of gods properly so-called in the minds of primitive peoples. That sweeping hypothesis is treated as an indubitable fact, and the elaborate explanations of it put forward by different and conflicting schools of rationalist anthropologists are for the most part illustrations of the principle *obscurum per obscurius.* Surely the intelligence with which these anthropologists insist on endowing primitive man, an intelligence sufficient to work out a belief in a beneficent Supreme Being from the personification of inanimate objects, or from ghosts of doubtful character, would have been more than sufficient to enable the savage to realise that ' the invisible things of him, from the creation of the world are clearly seen, being understood by the things that are made.'[1] The intelligence that could people ghostland with countless shadowy forms of headmen whose bodies had rotted in the grave, understood something of the nature of the vital

[1] Rom. i, 20.

principle animating man and of his eternal
destiny.

Sir James Frazer assures us that the savage would
as soon doubt his own conscious existence as doubt
the fact of his survival after death.[1] Furthermore,
Sir James testifies to the universality of this belief
among the savage races of mankind and, raising the
question as to the grounds of the belief, he answers
that as a matter of historical fact men seem to have
inferred the persistence of their personality after
death both from the phenomena of their inner life
and from the phenomena of the external world.[2]
Why then should they not have inferred the
existence of God in precisely the same way ? Yet
Sir James supposes that they first of all inferred a
number of gods ' who, behind the veil of nature, pull
the strings that set the vast machinery in motion,'
and, in course of time, becoming dissatisfied with
polytheism as an expression of the world, gradually
discarded it in favour of some unifying principle.

This, of course, is sheer guesswork. The only real
knowledge we possess of the psychology of the
primitive human mind is derived from the rapidly
disappearing savages of modern times, and they all,
without exception, believe in some kind of Supreme
Being, even though they may be at the same time
polytheists. The dogmatic assertions of rationalists
as to the mental states of really primitive man,
embody nothing more than prejudiced speculations.
The only available material on which a judgment
can be formed, the literature of ancient peoples, is

[1] *The Belief in Immortality*, Vol. I, p. 468.
[2] *Ibid.*, Vol. I, p. 217.

certainly not first-hand evidence since the literature was written long after the historic races had emerged from the primitive state. But the modern savage *is* a human document—and a document in conflict with rationalist theories.

An ever-increasing mass of evidence tends to show that the Supreme Being of savage creeds was not a later development from minor gods, but altogether anterior to them. For instance, Andrew Lang argues : ' If the All-Father belief, among savages, were the latest result of human speculation, we should expect it to be the most prominent and powerful. Far from being prominent, it is, in Australia, an esoteric belief, concealed from women, young boys, and uninitiated white men.' Again : ' Among other peoples, ancestor-worshippers and polytheists, sacrifice and service to ghosts and gods are highly conspicuous, while the Creative Being receives no sacrifice, or but " stinted sizings," and, often, is only the shadow of a name. He is therefore not the latest and brightest figure evolved by speculation, but precisely the reverse.'[1]

This overshadowing of the Supreme Being, in the popular worship, by lesser gods, ghosts, and spirits, seems to be a distinctive feature of all primitive religions. Thus, Réville, in a chapter on the Deities and Myths of Mexico, says : ' We have to observe that, by an inconsistency which again has its analogies in other religions, the cultus of the supreme deity and his consort was pretty much effaced in the popular devotions and practices by that of divinities

[1] *Encyclopædia of Religion and Ethics*, Vol. VI, Art. : God, Primitive and Savage.

who were perhaps less august, and in some cases
were even derived from the substance of the supreme
deity himself, but in any case seemed to stand
nearer to humanity than he did.'[1]

It is not at all clear how facts of this kind are to
be reconciled with the theory which holds the
Supreme Being to be the final product of evolution.
On the contrary, they seem to indicate that the
Supreme Being was the original concept of the
savage mind, especially as we find it admitted that
deities, in course of time, did tend to slip into the
background. ' Amongst other backward peoples of
the earth,' says Dr. Jevons, ' we find the names of
gods surviving, not only with no worship but with
no myths attached to them ;   and the inference
plainly is that, as they are still remembered to be
gods, they were once objects of worship certainly,
and probably once were subjects of mythology.'[2]

But, we are asked, how is it possible for pure
monotheism to have degenerated into polytheism ?
Surely the answer lies before us on the pages of the
Old Testament : because of the wickedness of men's
hearts. Even the Jews from time to time wandered
after strange gods, and those gods had been en-
throned by the same human passions which had
moved the Jews to abandon Jehovah.   Just as a
stream is purest at its source and gathers up defile-
ment on its way to the ocean, so in the course of
time did belief in the one true God become less pure,
and more adulterated with ideas which were of the

[1] *Origin and Growth of Religion as illustrated by the Native
Religions of Mexico and Peru,* by Albert Réville, p. 47.
[2] *The Idea of Gods in Early Religions,* by F. B. Jevons, p. 58.

earth earthy. The natural man, in his hates, his jealousies, his deceits, his thefts, could not expect the help of the God of Righteousness, and so in his perversity he turned to unseen superhuman powers who, he thought, might be cajoled or propitiated into helping in nefarious enterprises, for they were a venal rabble, these lesser gods and goddesses. Naturally, they were not conceived of as being altogether evil, but they were regarded as being on a decidedly lower moral plane than the Supreme Being. They were, perhaps, the outcome of a misunderstanding of some of the divine attributes by carnal-minded men. If it be urged further that this degeneration theory does not fit in with the evolutionary concept of the history of mankind, ever on the upward grade by minute steps or by enormous leaps, we can only reply that the evolutionary concept in this case does not fit the facts, and facts are stubborn things.

It would appear then that the evolution of the idea of God, whether from the spirits that ride the storm, or from ghostly ancestors, or from lesser gods, is by no means the established truth proclaimed by rationalists. Careful investigation leads the impartial enquirer to conclude that the idea of God did not evolve at all, but was gathered quite naturally, even by primitive man, from the consideration of the phenomena of nature around him for, as the mythology of the poets has it, the upper links of Nature's chain are fastened to Jupiter's throne.

PERSONAL IMMORTALITY

(Reprinted by Permission of the Catholic Truth Society)

' I THINK that one abstains from writing or printing on the immortality of the soul,' says Emerson in his famous essay on immortality, ' because, when he comes to the end of his statement, the hungry eyes that run through it will close disappointed ; the listeners say, that is not here which we desire ;—and I shall be as much wronged by their hasty conclusions, as they feel themselves wronged by my omissions. I mean that I am a better believer, and all serious souls are better believers in the immortality, than we can give grounds for.'[1]

If hungry eyes, after scrutinising the arguments for a life beyond the grave, close disappointed, it is not infrequently because they have strained after what is not even on the dim, distant horizon—an unexceptionable proof of the everlasting survival of all human souls from reason alone. But though there be no such proof, it is not true, of Christians at least, that we are better believers in immortality than we can give grounds for.

Emerson himself appears to have made ' the

[1] *Letters and Social Aims* (Emerson's Works, Vol. VIII, Riverside edition), p. 328.

venture of faith,' as William James acted upon a maybe, because he felt that the risk was a noble one. Nowhere does he show an understanding of the fact that ' the venture of faith ' is warranted by reason. ' We cannot prove our faith by syllogisms. The argument refuses to form in the mind,'[1] says Emerson, all unconscious that it is not in the least necessary for it to do so. All that we are called upon to do is to show the reasonableness of the grounds of our faith. The fact of a divine revelation being once established in Christian apologetics, we are logically justified in making our final appeal to that revelation to establish, in all its fullness, the doctrine of personal immortality.

But in our inquiry into the destiny of the human soul we can travel far indeed along the road of pure reason. It was Plato, amongst the philosophers of antiquity the great protagonist of man's immortality, who wrote ' Reason is for us King of Heaven and Earth.'[2]

Dr. Alger, as an appendix to his *Critical History of the Doctrine of a Future Life*, gives a bibliography of more than five thousand works dealing with his subject. A casual perusal of this bibliography makes it evident that the question of man's immortality has been considered from every conceivable angle. It is not the purport of this pamphlet to attempt any new argument, but rather to group and present the arguments for immortality that have swayed men's minds throughout the ages.

[1] *Letters and Social Aims* (Emerson's Works, Vol. VIII, Riverside edition), p. 328.
[2] *Philebus*, 28, C. νοῦς ἐστὶ βασιλεὺς ἡμῖν οὐρανοῦ τε καὶ γῆς.

D

I

The main argument for the immortality of the human soul arises from a consideration of the nature of that soul. The term ' soul ' is used in many different senses both in philosophy and in every-day life. Here, however, it is used to designate ' the subject of our mental life, the ultimate principle by which we feel, think, and will.'[1] Qualities cannot inhere without a subject ; and just as physical attributes imply a body, so spiritual attributes imply a soul.

When we say that a material object—a pyramid or a pebble or a human body—perishes, we do not mean that the material object is reduced to nothingness, goes out of being ; we mean that it has altered its form of being. Science tells us that every particle of the pyramid, or the pebble, or the human body, is still in the physical universe. But it has lost its individuality, and therefore we say it has ceased to exist. There are only two conceivable ways in which it can cease to exist ; either because of the separation of the parts of which it is composed, or because of the dissolution of the parts of some other thing upon which it depends for its existence. For instance, if the bricks that go to make up a wall are blown to pieces by a shell, the wall itself is destroyed ; but the iridescent colours of a soap-bubble vanish, not because of the disintegration of their parts, but because of the bursting of the bubble in which they inhere.

Now, is it possible for the human soul to perish,

[1] *Psychology*, by Fr. Maher, S.J., 2nd edition, p. 443.

after the manner of material things, in either of these ways ? Only if it were a substance like the wall, an aggregate of atoms possessing extension, could it perish by the dissolution of parts. And that it is not in any sense a conglomeration of parts is abundantly clear from a consideration of its actions. Thus we are able to form ideas not merely of the individual things—Peter, a river, a judge, but also the corresponding abstract ideas of man, water, justice. Clearly, then, there must be within us a faculty capable of *abstracting* from the particular characteristics of material things, of disengaging the thing from its material setting, of completely stripping it of all material conditions.

That faculty cannot be material. It is impossible even to conceive such a thing. For in that case, the idea would occupy space, and correspond part by part with the organ apprehending it. Hence St. Thomas Aquinas says : ' If the understanding were a corporeal substance, intelligible ideas of things would be received in it only as representing individual things. At that rate the understanding would have no conception of the universal, but only of the particular, which is manifestly false.'[1] The fact, then, of our being able to form abstract or universal ideas is, in itself, a proof of the immateriality, or, as it is technically called, the spirituality of the soul, a proof that the soul is, in its essence, independent of matter.

But we can do more than apprehend ideas. We can compare ideas when apprehended, and form a

[1] *Contra Gentiles* (trans. by Fr. Rickaby, S.J.), Book II, c. xlix, p. 3.

judgment as to their compatibility or incompati-
bility. This implies that the soul is one undivided
entity. Thus, in the judgment 'the soul is immortal,' there are two distinct ideas which are
simultaneously apprehended, compared, and pronounced compatible. The comparison would be
impossible if the concept of ' soul ' were in one part
of the mind, and the concept ' immortal ' in another.
A third part could not compare them, because it
would know nothing of either, and obviously they
could not compare themselves any more than if they
were ideas in the minds of two distinct individuals.
If both ideas were in each part of the mind there
would be a duality of judgments, which is, manifestly, contrary to our experience. The fact, then,
that a judgment is made is a proof that the mind
has no parts, that the soul is, in philosophical
language, simple, i.e. devoid of composition. Yet we
have only considered a very simple mental operation. Not only can the mind compare ideas and
form judgments, but it can compare judgments
and form inferences. It can, for instance, compare
the judgments ' all men are animals ' and ' Peter is
a man,' and draw the conclusion ' *therefore* Peter is
an animal.' How explain this mental process on the
supposition that the different ideas and different
judgments are in different mental compartments ?
It is utterly incomprehensible except on the hypothesis that the soul is one indivisible agent.

Or consider the marvellous power of reflection
which the mind possesses. I can think of myself,
and I can proceed to think of myself thinking of
myself, recognising meanwhile the absolute identity

between the ' I ' that thinks and the ' I ' that is
thought of. The mind completely doubles back
upon itself, and inspects itself. But it is utterly
impossible for the bodily eye to look at itself, never
mind looking at itself inspecting itself. Such an
action would be in direct opposition to the very
nature of matter. A knife cannot cut itself, a brush
cannot brush itself. By no possibility can an
extended body double back upon itself, and act upon
itself. Part of it may act upon part of it, but the
whole of it cannot act upon the whole of it. Yet
this is precisely what the soul does—thus forcing
upon us the conclusion that it is in no way extended,
that it has no parts. ' Of no bodily substance,' says
St. Thomas Aquinas, ' is the action turned back
upon the agent. But the understanding in its action
does reflect and turn round upon itself : for as it
understands an object, so also it understands that it
does understand, and so endlessly. Hence Holy
Scripture calls intelligent subsistent beings by the
name of " spirits," using of them the style which it is
wont to use for the incorporeal Deity. . . .'[1]

Again, as we review the emotional experiences of
our lives, it is impossible for us to doubt that we are
the same persons who were thrilled by them. ' Man
says " I " in all the phases of his existence. When a
little heedless child, whose vivid fancy roves like
a butterfly over the flowers of life, he was I ; when
a boy, and seeing the roads of life open out before
him he chose that on which he should fix his steps,
he was I ; when a young man and he struggled in
the combat and cried out, " O my God ! save me, I

[1] *Contra Gentiles* (trans. by Fr. Rickaby, S.J.), xlix. 7 and 8.

perish," he was I ; when a grown man, and he begins to understand the nothingness of human things, and to open his ears to the rapid steps of the coming eternity, he is I ; when an old man, who, in a few years, lamenting his mistakes and hoping in the mercy of God, will daily look for the end of his miseries, he will be I—always I—the same, the unchangeable I.'[1]

How are we to account for this abiding identity of personality ? Not on the grotesque theory that the mind is composed of successive mental states, for successive mental states of themselves have no more connection with each other than successive flashes of lightning.   And assuredly not on the assumption that our bodily organism is the subject of our mental states, for ' in a few months (not in seven years, as was formerly thought) our body is entirely renewed. None of the flesh of our body existed three months ago ; the shoulders, face, eyes, mouth, the arms, the hair—all our organism is but a current of molecules, a ceaselessly renewed flame, a river which we may look upon all our lives, but never see the same water again.'[2] Only on the hypothesis of an abiding indivisible principle underlying our fleeting mental states can we account for the manifest unity of consciousness.

It is clear then that the soul is not composed of parts, and therefore cannot perish by being resolved into constituents.   Furthermore, since it has been shown to be immaterial, independent of matter, it cannot perish on account of the dissolution of the body.   The obvious fact that the soul is in some way

[1] Monsabré, *Confer.* xvi., p. 176.
[2] Camille Flammarion in *The Proofs of Life after Death* (edited by R. J. Thompson), p. 97.

dependent on the body led the Epicurean Lucretius, in the first century B.C., to formulate an argument that is still part of the stock-in-trade of the Materialist : ' The soul is born with the body, it grows and decays with the body, therefore it perishes with the body.'[1]

As we have seen, abstract ideas, intellectual judgment, logical inference, and the act of reflection are the outcome of purely spiritual actions, and indicate that the soul is *essentially* independent of matter, and therefore essentially independent of the body ; nevertheless, in some of its operations it is extrinsically dependent on the body. It is only through the senses of the body that we receive impressions of external objects. These impressions in turn stimulate the imagination to form mental images of the objects, and it is from the mental images thus formed that the mind abstracts ideas. In the present state of the soul's actuating the body, and operating through the body, the bodily organs furnish the material, the data, as it were, for the mind's operations, but it does not follow that the mind cannot act unless material be provided in that way.

The brain is not the ' organ of mind ' in the sense in which the eye is the organ of sight. The eye is necessary precisely in order that we may see ; the brain is necessary, not precisely in order that the mind may think, but in order that the mind may be provided with the mental image, which is a necessary condition for its action in this life. Thought is not, as Materialists allege, essentially bound up with brain. On this point Dr. McTaggart, Fellow and Lecturer of Trinity College, Cambridge, writes : ' With

[1] *De Rerum Natura*, Lib. III. vv. 446 *seq.*

regard to the connexion of the brain with thought,
the chief evidence for it appears to be that
diseases or mutilations of the brain affect the course
of thought. But this does not prove that, even while
a man has a brain, his thoughts are directly connected with it. Many things are capable of disturb-
ing thought, which are not essential to existence.
For example, a sufficiently severe attack of toothache may render all consecutive abstract thought
impossible. But if the tooth was extracted, I should
still be able to think. And, in the same way, the
fact that an abnormal state of the brain may affect
our thoughts does not prove that the normal states
of the brain are necessary for thought.

' Even if the brain be essential to thought while we
have bodies, it would not follow that when we
ceased to have brains we could not think without
them. The same argument applies here as with the
organs of sense. It might be that the present in-
ability of the self to think except in connection with
the body was a limitation which was imposed by the
presence of the body, and which vanished with it.'[1]
The utter illogicality of the Lucretian argument that
' when the brain is out, the man would die and there
an end ' is illustrated by this very striking analogy.
' If a man is shut in a house, the transparency of the
windows is an essential condition of his seeing the
sky. But it would not be prudent to infer that, if
he walked out of the house, he could not see the sky
because there was no longer any glass through which
he might see it.'[2]

[1] *Some Dogmas of Religion*, by Dr. McTaggart, pp. 105, 106.
[2] *Ibid.*, p. 105.

The soul then does not perish with the body as the subject of its inherence, and as we have already seen that, having no constituent parts, it cannot perish by dissolution, it follows that it is, *of its own nature, incorruptible.* Thus the really vital question raised by Philosophy—does the soul survive the body ? is answered by Philosophy—the soul does survive the body ; the death of the body is not the end of all, there is a life beyond.

There is only one other conceivable way in which the soul could cease to exist—by annihilation. Just as creation is the production of an entity from nothingness, so annihilation is the reduction of an entity to nothingness. Creation and annihilation are co-relative terms, so that as only Omnipotence can create, only Omnipotence can annihilate. Reason, apart from Revelation, gives us an assurance that annihilation cannot be the ultimate fate of the soul. The nature of the thing created is surely an indication of the intention of its creator, and the soul is, of its own nature, incorruptible. We may well ask, Would an all-wise God have created a soul of an incorruptible nature, to perish more completely and utterly than the corruptible body that it animates ?

> Can it be ?
> Matter immortal ? and shall spirit die ?
> Above the nobler, shall less noble rise ?
> Shall man alone, for whom all else revives,
> No resurrection know ? Shall man alone,
> Imperial man ! be sown in barren ground,
> Less privileged than grain on which he feeds ?[1]

But we have the guarantee of Revelation that it is not God's intention ever to annihilate the soul :

[1] *Night Thoughts*, by Edward Young, Night the Sixth, p. 114 (Nelson's edition), 1856.

' And these shall go into everlasting punishment ;
but the just into life everlasting.'[1]   The sentence
that Christ will pass upon the wicked is in itself a
proof of the natural immortality of the soul.   For if
immortality were not natural to the soul, God would
have to endow it with immortality in order to punish
it for ever—an act that it would be blasphemous to
attribute to the Deity.

Objections are raised against both parts of the
philosophical proof of the soul's survival.   On the
one hand, it is urged that the soul is composite, and
therefore perishes as everything in the world
perishes, by the separation of the parts of which it is
composed :   on the other hand, a crude Materialism
battles against man's immortality with a jaw-bone-
of-an-ass sort of weapon, by insisting that mind is
a phase of matter, or a function of matter, which
may be pounded out of existence in a mortar.

An example of the first kind of objection is to
hand in the Rationalist Press Association's manual
by E. S. P. Haynes, who says of the unity of consciousness :   ' If one closely examines that doctrine,
the unity is more apparent than real.   A man's
memory only begins, properly speaking, with adolescence, and even then it is very faint.   He is constantly unable to recollect something which he
wishes to recollect, and has to wait on the chance of
the brain suddenly throwing up what he wants from
a great mass of what we call unconscious cerebration
below.   His memory, and in fact all his consciousness as we know it, are entirely at the mercy of
drugs and anæsthetics and a proper supply of food.'[2]

[1] Matt. xxv, 46.   [2] *The Belief in Personal Immortality*, p. 67.

Now an examination of the *nature* of the unity of consciousness, so far from showing that unity to be only apparent, makes it evident that the unity is so real that it amounts to an absolute identity of personality, an identity without parallel in the order of Nature. It has been compared, by thinkers of the same school as Mr. Haynes, to the identity of a regiment, or a candle flame, or a river. One moment's reflection is sufficient to show that in these latter cases there is only an apparent unity such as Mr. Haynes has in mind, but which bears no resemblance whatsoever to the unity of consciousness. Do the men of a regiment recognize themselves as being identical with the men of sixty years ago ? Is the flame of a candle that has been lit ten minutes numerically the same as the flame that appeared when the match was put to the wick ? Is a river ever identical at any two moments ? In sixty years' time every man in the regiment is replaced by a totally different man, whilst the flame and the stream are continuously fed by ever-changing matter. Nothing remains the same.

But an entirely new element forces itself upon our attention when we consider the unity of consciousness. Here, though the whole physical organism is in a state of constant flux, no less than the regiment, or the flame, or the stream, the same conscious personality persists throughout, holding in each successive moment all the changes of the past.

We have here not only a real unity, but an absolute identity transcending the properties of matter. We may replace one string of a violin by another exactly similar to it, and when the second

string is played upon it gives the same note as the
first.   But, supposing, on any theory of 'mind-
stuff,' that the strings are capable of cognition, can
the second string know that the first gave that
note ?   How can it, seeing that it is an entirely
different string ?   Now it is certain that the molecular
structure of the brain of a man of thirty-five has
completely altered since he was twenty-five.   Yet
the brain reacts in the same way to the same
stimulus as it did when he was twenty-five, and a
similar mental state results.   But the physically
renovated brain can no more remember the former
mental state than the second string of the violin can
remember the sound given by the first.   Yet the
former mental state *is* remembered, and the subsequent state recognized as similar to it.   Clearly
there must be something within the man remaining
always the same, an abiding principle—an absolute
unity of consciousness.

When Mr. Haynes writes of ' the *brain* suddenly
throwing up what he wants,' we begin to understand why he finds the unity of ' consciousness '
more apparent than real.   It looks as though he had
made his close examination of consciousness with a
scalpel.   The startlingly original theory that ' a
man's memory only begins, properly speaking, with
adolescence,' the reader can put to the practical test
of his own experience.   Psychology is not so bank-
rupt in explanations of the phenomenon of forgetting
that we need, with Mr. Haynes, throw up both
hands at the caprice of the ' brain.'[1]   Somehow the

[1] See *The Psychopathology of Everyday Life*, by S. Freud
(trans. Brill), chaps. i, ii, iii, iv, vii.

one point that really matters seems to have escaped
Mr. Haynes' notice. No matter how much a man
may forget, if he can call up at will *one single memory*
of his childhood's days—and who cannot ?—that
fact alone argues an abiding personal identity
between the grown man and the child—the *real*
unity of consciousness which Mr. Haynes impugns.
That fact alone is the death-warrant of Materialistic
theories of memory. The helplessness of Materialism
in the presence of such a fact is well brought out by
Dr. Alger :

'A photographic image impressed on suitable
paper and then obliterated is restored by exposure
to the fumes of mercury. But if an indefinite
number of impressions were superimposed on the
same paper, could the fumes of mercury restore any
one called for at random ? Yet man's memory is a
plate with a hundred millions of impressions all
clearly preserved, and he can at will select and
evoke the one he wants. No conceivable relationship of materialistic forces can account for the facts
of this miraculous daguerreotype-plate of experience,
and the power of the mind to call out into solitary
conspicuousness a desired picture which has forty-
nine million nine hundred and ninety-nine thousand
nine hundred and ninety-nine latent pictures lying
above it, and fifty millions below it.'[1]

Crude Materialism found systematic expression in
the writings of Pierre Gassendi[2] about the middle of

[1] *A Critical History of the Doctrine of a Future Life*, 10th
edition, p. 628.
[2] *De Vita Epicuri* (1647) ; *Syntagma Philosophiæ Epicureæ*
(1649).

the seventeenth century, and came to maturity in the *Système de la Nature* of Holbach (1770). In this country Hobbes, Hartley, and Priestley made desultory efforts to explain mental phenomena on materialistic lines, but it was left for the German philosopher Vogt to attempt a psychology without a soul, and on physiological lines define thought as a secretion of the brain. Following in his wake, Büchner produced his *Kraft und Stoff* (Force and Matter), which has been aptly described as ' the Bible of German Materialism.'

The soul is, in Büchner's conception, simply a product of matter : ' In the same manner as the steam-engine produces motion, so does the organic complication of force-endowed materials produce in the animal body effects so interwoven as to become a unit, which is then by us called spirit, soul, thought.'[1] A little reflection makes it obvious that Büchner has simply jumped the difficulty. If he tells us that in the same manner as the steam-engine produces physical motion, the animal body produces physical motion, we can understand him—because all the terms are homogeneous. But, as has been explained, thought is, in its essence, completely independent of the molecular motion of the brain. Thought and molecular motion are heterogeneous—have nothing in common—and to account for thought by accounting for molecular motion is to beg the whole question. Thought and matter, as John Stuart Mill has said, are ' not merely different, but are at the opposite poles of existence,'[2] and

[1] *Kraft und Stoff* (trans.), p. 135.
[2] *Essays on Religion*, p. 202.

Büchner's analogy is in reality an attempt to jump unobserved from pole to pole. Besides, the steam-engine analogy leaves out the engineer ; does he, asks Dr. Alger, ' nimbly leap off and immortally escape ' ?[1]

Huxley's view is hardly less crude than Büchner's. ' Thought,' said Huxley, ' is as much a function of matter as motion is.'[2] The word *function*, like the word Mesopotamia, has a comforting sound, and in addition rejoices in a bewildering variety of meanings. Enough has been said to show that thought is not a product of matter—the description of it as a function of matter is only a subtle attempt to show that it is.

As William James has pointed out, if the word function be taken in any other sense, the case of the Materialist against immortality falls to the ground :

' When we think of the law that thought is a function of the brain we are not required to think of productive function only : *we are entitled also to consider permissive or transmissive function*. And this the ordinary psycho-physiologist leaves out of his account,'[3] with the result that he denies the simplicity and spirituality of the soul, and consequently its immortality. But (continues Professor James) ' the fatal consequence is not coercive, the conclusion which materialism draws being due solely to its one-sided way of taking the word function. And, whether we care or not for immortality in itself, we ought, as mere critics doing police duty

[1] *A Critical History of the Doctrine of a Future Life*, 10th edition, p. 630.   [2] *Macmillan's Magazine*, May, 1870.
[3] *Human Immortality*, by William James, p. 32.

among the vagaries of mankind, to insist on the illogicality of a denial based on the flat ignoring of a palpable alternative.   How much more ought we to insist, as lovers of truth, when the denial is that of such a vital hope of mankind.   In strict logic, then, the fangs of cerebralistic materialism are drawn.'[1]

II

' The notion of the survival of the spirit after death in some form, whether clear or vague,' says Henry Frank, ' has ever existed in the human mind from the most primitive times to the present hour.'[2] All attempts to minimise the universality of that belief have failed ignominiously.   Yet the Rationalist Press Association still pins its faith to Haeckel's sweeping declaration :

' The belief in immortality is not found in Buddhism, the religion that dominates thirty per cent of the entire human race ;   it is not found in the ancient popular religion of the Chinese, nor in the reformed religion of Confucius, which succeeded it ; and, what is still more significant, it is not found in the earlier and purer religion of the Jews.'[3]

This passage is quoted with approval by Mr. Haynes in the R.P.A. manual, *The Belief in Personal Immortality*, p. 69.   On the same page there is a reference to Sir J. G. Frazer's classical work, *The Belief in Immortality*, which makes one wonder if

[1] *Human Immortality*, pp. 39, 40.
[2] *Modern Light on Immortality*, by Henry Frank, p. 35.
[3] *The Riddle of the Universe*, p. 199.

Mr. Haynes is altogether unaware of the fact that Frazer's views are in direct antagonism to Haeckel's. Thus Frazer says : ' The question whether our conscious personality survives after death has been answered by almost all races of men in the affirmative. On this point sceptical or agnostic peoples are nearly, if not wholly, unknown.'[1] To Buddhism in particular, Frazer, in common with Max Müller, Rhys Davids, and other competent scholars, attributes ' a belief in the existence of the human soul after death.'[2]

Mr. Haynes does not seem to have read Metchnikoff's trenchant exposure of the glaring inaccuracies of Haeckel in the very passage cited in the R.P.A. manual.[3] Metchnikoff, himself an opponent of personal immortality, after careful investigation, arrives at the conclusion that Buddhism ' is so persuaded of survival after death as being the rule, that it grants only to rare and elect souls the privilege of at length laying down the burden of continuous life.'[4] He quotes Réville for the statement that the Chinese race as a whole ' fully recognise the conception of personal survival after death.'[5] How wide of the mark Haeckel is with regard to Confucius may be gathered from a perusal of some of the latter's recorded statements. Thus :

' Death is not destruction properly so-called, but a decomposition which resolves each substance into

---

[1] *The Belief in Immortality* (Gifford Lectures, 1911–1912), by J. G. Frazer, Vol. I, p. 33.   [2] *Ibid.*, p. 26.
[3] See *The Nature of Man* (1916 edition), pp. 144–60.
[4] *Ibid.*, p. 148.
[5] *Histoire des Religions*, Vol. III, La religion chinoise.

its natural state. The intellectual substance again ascends to heaven from which it came, the animal spirit, *khi*, unites with the aerial fluid, and the terrestrial and aqueous substances turn once more to earth and water.'[1]

As for the Jews, contrast Haeckel's dogmatic assertion with the calm, impartial verdict of Hastings Rashdall : ' The Jews were at one time behind the other nations in the distinctness of their belief in personal immortality, just because (it would seem) of the intensity with which they believed that obedience to Jehovah's laws would be rewarded by national victory and agricultural prosperity—a belief ultimately shattered by the experiences of the exile.'[2] On the whole, it would seem that, in this matter of the belief of mankind in immortality, as in others, Haeckel allowed his zeal in the cause of Materialism to get the better of his discretion.

With regard to the savage tribes, alleged to have no conception of a future life, we may safely say of them what Tylor says of the tribes alleged to have no religion : ' The case is in some degree similar to that of the tribes asserted to exist without language or without the use of fire. . . . As a matter of fact, the tribes are not found.'[3] Frazer thus expresses his considered judgment :

' It is impossible not to be struck by the strength, and perhaps we may say the universality, of the

---

[1] *Modern Light on Immortality*, p. 37.
[2] *The Theory of Good and Evil*, by Hastings Rashdall, Vol. II, pp. 217, 218.
[3] *Primitive Culture*, Vol. I, p. 378.

natural belief in immortality among the savage races of mankind. With them a life after death is not a matter of speculation and conjecture, of hope and fear ; it is a practical certainty which the individual as little dreams of doubting as he doubts the reality of his conscious existence.'[1]

Emerson forestalls the objection that the beliefs of various nations are puzzling in their diversity. ' I know well,' he says, ' that where this belief once existed it would necessarily take a base form for the savage and a pure form for the wise ;—so that I only look on the counterfeit as a proof that the genuine faith has been there.'[2]   It would be strange indeed if, amongst rude and barbarous peoples, the conception of a future life did not include many crudities and absurdities ; strange indeed if the Egyptian and the Zoroastrian conceived the same idea of heaven.   The really wonderful thing is that, despite all the diversity of concept, the same underlying belief in a life beyond the grave is always present.

Whence comes this universal belief ? Frazer raises the question, and answers it :

' What then is the kind of experience from which the theory of human immortality is deduced ? Is it our experience of the operations of our minds ? or is it our experience of external nature ? As a matter of historical fact—and you will remember that I am treating the question purely from the historical

---

[1] *The Belief in Immortality*, Vol. I, p. 468.
[2] *Letters and Social Aims* (Emerson's Works, Vol. VIII, Riverside edition), p. 308.

standpoint—men seem to have inferred the persistence of their personality after death both from the one kind of experience and from the other, that is, both from the phenomena of their inner life and from the phenomena of what we call the external world.'[1]

Clearly, then, the universal belief in the immortality of the human soul is not, as frequently stated, on all fours with the one-time universal belief in the sun's going round the earth.   The latter belief was based solely on observation of external phenomena, and could not be checked by comparison with the phenomena of man's inner life.   Moreover, it made no difference to man's life whether the sun went round the earth or vice versa.   It was not a question vitally affecting him—he had no personal practical interest in its solution.   But the question of immortality does vitally affect him—there is no man who does not want to know, no man who does not strive to know, the answer.   It is, in fact, *the* question of questions, upon his attitude to which the whole tenor of a man's life depends.

It is argued, therefore, that if, in such circumstances, the universal belief of mankind could be a mere delusion, human reason would be essentially fallacious, and incapable of ever attaining, with certainty, to truth.   Hence Dr. Quackenbos says : ' A psychological proof of post-mortem existence has been found in the fact that immortality is an apprehension of human reason.'[2]

---

[1] *The Belief in Immortality*, Vol. I, p. 217.
[2] *Body and Spirit*, by J. D. Quackenbos, p. 262.   See also p. 269.

Certainly the argument from the common consent of mankind is regarded by many opponents of the doctrine of personal immortality as being the most formidable. Thus in Metchnikoff's recently reprinted work *The Nature of Man*, the whole chapter on the immortality of the soul is in reality an attempt at undermining the force of this argument. So, too, Mr. Haynes, who, after devoting one chapter to the beliefs of savages and another to the beliefs of Egypt, Greece, and Rome, ultimately, *pace* Haeckel, can urge no stronger objection than that ' the Animistic belief in immortality includes every possible variety of opinion.'[1]

It would seem as though those who oppose man's immortality on so-called scientific grounds feel the sting of Professor Gase-Des Fosses' astute remark concerning the argument from common consent :

' If the name of science is given especially to all research based on facts, it can be said that this argument in favour of the immortality of the soul has a scientific value, as all its strength lies in establishing a fact which is universally human.'[2]

III

Aristotle, ' the master of those that know,'[3] formulated a maxim that has come to rank with the axioms of Euclid : ' *Nature does nothing in vain.*'[4] The astronomer, the geologist, the botanist, the

---

[1] *The Belief in Personal Immortality*, p. 69.
[2] *The Proofs of Life after Death* (compiled and edited by R. J. Thompson), p. 206.
[3] Dante's *Inferno*, canto iv. l. 131.
[4] *De Anima*, III. ix. 6. φύσις μήτε ποιεῖ μάτην μηθέν.

biologist, and the other searchers into the secrets of Nature, each in his own line, bears witness to the truth of Aristotle's dictum.

Nothing is purposeless in creation. Sturmius of old recommended an examination of the eye as a cure for Atheism, and Paley in his *Natural Theology* demonstrated how admirably every fibre in the eye fulfills its function.[1] What is true of the eye is true of the whole human body, and of every organic body. The lowest micro-organism is replete with purpose, with a teleology, a finality, ultimately traceable to the instincts, appetites, or desires that set the organism in motion. For ' the implanting of a desire indicates that the gratification of that desire is in the constitution of the creature that feels it ; the wish for food, the wish for motion, the wish for sleep, for society, for knowledge, are not random whims, but grounded in the structure of the creature, and meant to be satisfied by food, by motion, by sleep, by society, by knowledge.'[2]

But man, the lord of creation, has a soul above these things—above all created things. It is the daily lesson of his life that nothing finite ever satisfies his yearnings. From the child who covets a sixpenny toy to the miser who sets his heart on coffers of glittering gold, no one is happy when he has attained the object of all his ceaseless craving, of all his restless seeking. ' Some measure of happiness is attainable in this life, but not perfect and true happiness,' says St. Thomas Aquinas. ' For happiness, inasmuch as it is a perfect and sufficient good,

---

[1] *The Works of William Paley* (1839 edition), pp. 439–41, 451.
[2] *Letters and Social Aims* (Riverside edition), p. 320.

excludes all evil and satisfies all desire. But the exclusion of all evil is impossible in this life, fraught as it is with many inevitable evils—ignorance, inordinate desire, bodily inflictions. . . . So, too, the desire for good cannot be satisfied in this life. For man naturally desires permanence in the good that he possesses, whereas the good things of this life are transitory ; life itself, which we naturally desire and wish to continue for ever, instinctively shrinking from death, is itself fleeting. Whence it is impossible to attain to true happiness in this life.'[1]

Yet it is precisely perfect happiness—happiness unalloyed and unending—that man craves ; the very happiness that we have seen to be unattainable in this life. If then there be no life beyond the grave, the highest and noblest aspiration of man is meaningless, purposeless, implanted within him merely to be frustrated, alone of all things in Nature ' in vain.' We scale the ladder of creation only to find it break at the topmost rung ! That is indeed ' a slaughter-house style of thinking.'

But, it is contended, the desire for perfect happiness does fulfil its purpose in this life—in stimulating man to effort, presumably in much the same way as a wisp of hay placed beyond a donkey's reach induces that animal to keep going. The search after the chimerical philosopher's stone of old resulted in much scientific lore ; so, too, it is urged, man's striving after the will-o'-the-wisp of perfect happiness has brought about the advancement of civilization, and is, in fact, the very mainspring of progress.

There would be more force in this argument if

[1] *Summa Theologica*, Prima Secundæ, Quæstio V. Art. II.

those who urge it really did attribute the progress of the human race to the belief in immortality.   But what do we actually find ?   The Utilitarianism that justifies the argument has been described by Mr. Lecky as being ' profoundly immoral,' in the sense of not recognizing the function of religious beliefs as factors in social evolution.   ' Cease to look beyond the stars for your hopes and rewards,' says Nietzsche, in a fine frenzy for the evolution of the Superman. And has it not been a favourite taunt that the doctrine of a future life taught men how to die, instead of how to live as members of society ?   Even Professor Frazer is at some pains to explain that the belief in a life beyond the grave has been responsible for many degrading crimes, thus retarding the moral development of the savage.   Metchnikoff, so far from thinking that the belief in immortality has led to the advancement of knowledge, contends that the advancement of knowledge has killed the belief in immortality :   ' It is easy to see why the advance of knowledge has diminished the numbers of believers in the persistence of consciousness after death, and that complete annihilation at death is the conception accepted by the vast majority of enlightened persons.'[1]

Now if ' the vast majority of enlightened persons ' have got at the back of the ' illusion ' of immortality, how, we may well ask, can that ' illusion,' recognized as such, stimulate enlightened persons to effort ?   If the donkey *knew* that the wisp of hay was hopelessly out of his reach, would he still continue to follow it ?

It would appear then that, whatever may have

[1] *The Nature of Man*, p. 161.

been the case in the barbarous past, in this enlightened age the universal desire of man for a future life
has no *raison d'être* whatever. Even with regard to
the past, we cannot allow the advocates of annihilation to have it both ways. If the desire for a future
life has acted as a check on the intellectual and moral
development of mankind, clearly that desire does not
find its justification in the progress of the human race.

Nor would it, if it had brought about all the progress of our boasted civilisation. The desire is for
perfect happiness, and nothing short of perfect
happiness satisfies it. The only justification of that
desire is the possibility of its fulfilment. To argue
that it is satisfactorily accounted for by the benefits
that it has brought to man in this life, is about as
sensible as to account for the quacking of geese by
the fact that this noise, acting as an alarm-signal,
saved the Roman Capitol.

There is no escape—the man who denies personal
immortality must deny also what Sir Thomas Browne
described as ' the only indisputable axiom in
philosophy,'[1] *Nature does nothing in vain.*

IV

Of Kant, Mr. E. S. P. Haynes is scornful, for that
his ' belief in immortality was ultimately based on
nothing more than a belief in the moral government
of the world.'[2] He does not censure Kant for rejecting the metaphysical consideration of the question
on the ground that from Pure Reason nothing is

---

[1] *Religio Medici*, Part I, sect. XV.
[2] *The Belief in Personal Immortality*, p. 54.

trustworthy, though we might have expected a Rationalist to utter a word of protest against that standpoint.   Kant's unforgivable sin, in the eyes of Mr. Haynes, is that he insisted on the immortality of the soul as a postulate of Practical Reason.   According to Kant, man has no alternative to belief in immortality except the impossible one of acting against his rational nature.   His argument has been summarised thus : ' The law of duty demands moral perfection or holiness.   But this is impossible in our present life, therefore it can only be attained by an indefinite progress, and this progress is only possible under the hypothesis of an existence and a personality that are indefinitely prolonged.'[1]   Stripped of its formality, the same argument is advanced by Von Hartmann : ' The bare fact that we possess moral instincts is, even taken by itself, the refutation of all anti-teleological views of the universe.'[2]

The argument in itself is sound—it is not in any way essential to it to admit, with Kant, the *autonomy of reason*.   The force of the argument lies in the *obligation* of man to act in consonance with the dictates of reason, and this is none the less true when the obligation is radicated in something more fundamental than reason.

Reason cannot be the ultimate source of the obligation, since reason cannot be a law unto itself. A law implies two distinct persons—the lawgiver who commands and the subject who obeys.   A ruler cannot give a law to himself, since every law is a

[1] *A History of the Problems of Philosophy*, by Janet and Séailles, trans. by Ada Monahan, Vol. II, p. 371.
[2] *D. sittl. Bewusstsein*, p. 465.

command, an act of jurisdiction of one person over another. It is therefore impossible for reason to be at once ruler and ruled. Granted that there is an external legislator, whose law is promulgated to man by reason, and the moral argument for the immortality of the soul is beyond rebuttal.

Nature dictates to us that it is to our best interests to do what is right and avoid what is wrong. But unless there be a future life, it is not at all clear how such a line of conduct is to our best interests. Virtue is oftentimes its own reward, but oftentimes it is not. What of the countless thousands who have sacrificed their lives on the battlefield at the call of duty ? Nature prompted them to answer that call, and, if a soldier's grave be the end of all, then, indeed, are the dictates of Nature self-stultifying. ' Only if we suppose that the present life of human beings has an end which lies in part beyond the limits of the present natural order, in so far as that order is accessible to present human observation, can we find a rational meaning and explanation for human life as we see it ; and by far the most natural and intelligible form of such a world-end is the belief in Immortality for the individual souls which have lived there.'[1]

It has been objected to this argument that a realisation of the excellence of virtue in itself would dull its edge. In the language of Mr. Haynes it ' quite ignores the contention that morality is of a higher type when it is not based on rewards and punishments.'[2] Yet Kant, to whom it appealed

---

[1] *The Theory of Good and Evil*, by H. Rashdall, Vol. II, p. 215.
[2] *The Belief in Personal Immortality*, p. 68.

with overwhelming force, was the Apostle of ' Independent Morality,' which sought to establish right
and wrong without any regard for rewards and
punishments, without regard even to the natural
consequences of man's actions. As a matter of fact,
the argument has always gone hand in hand with a
keen appreciation of virtue for its own sake. Unless
there be a keen appreciation of the excellence of
virtue, it is impossible to argue that because ' in this
life only distant approaches to the true ideal are
possible to the best, there must be a hereafter in which
a progressively closer approximation to it should be
possible.'[1]

The argument is in reality an obvious corollary to
the rationality of the Universe, and it was on this
ground that it won the reasoned assent of Rousseau.
' If,' said he, ' I had no other proof of the immortality
of the soul than the prosperity of the wicked and the
oppression of the just in this world, that alone would
be enough to convince me. I would feel constrained
to explain such a manifest contradiction, such a
terrible exception to the established harmony of the
universe. I would be forced to exclaim within
myself, '' All cannot end with death. All will be put
into proper order and harmony after death.'' '

The point is important. Failure to realise that the
question of man's immortality is part and parcel of
the larger question of the rationality of the Universe
has led Mr. Haynes to say, of a belief in the moral
government of the world : ' This has by now become
a great prop to thinkers who believe in immortality,
and who prefer not to tackle the problem on its own

[1] *The Theory of Good and Evil*, Vol. II, p. 266.

merits.'[1] Surely one shining merit of the doctrine of
immortality is that it enables us to give a rational
account of the Universe at large. It is impossible
to divorce the two questions. ' The deeper our conviction of the rationality of the Universe,' says
Rashdall, ' the stronger becomes our unwillingness
to believe that such an order can be final and permanent. Hence it is that a sincere Theism has nearly
always carried with it a belief in Immortality.'[2]

Mr. Haynes, by way of showing that the doctrine
of the moral government of the world ' can scarcely
be accepted without question,' presents us with this
engaging story : ' My eldest daughter, when four
years old, was told at school that the Almighty was
a kind personage who looked after children and little
birds with a care that never failed. No sooner had
she arrived home than she saw the cat devour a
sparrow in the garden ! She was naturally impressed
with the idea that the divine government of the
world was marked by a certain carelessness which
she deplored, even when she was told that many cats
would starve if they did not eat birds.'[3] We would
be interested to know how Mr. Haynes, having
cleared his little daughter's mind of the idea of the
moral government of the world, explained to her its
rationality. On this subject he says never a word.
The difficulty as to why Providence permits sparrows
to be eaten by cats is not generally regarded as in-
surmountable, and fades into insignificance beside
others, much more pertinent to the present question,

[1] *The Belief in Personal Immortality*, p. 54.
[2] *The Theory of Good and Evil*, Vol. II, p. 217.
[3] *The Belief in Personal Immortality*, p. 55.

of which Mr. Haynes has apparently never heard. He might, for instance, address himself to the main difficulty against his view, as stated by Hastings Rashdall :

' On the supposition of universal mortality the contrast between the capacities of human nature and its actual destiny, between the immensity of the man's outlook and the limitations of his actual horizon, between the splendour of his ideals and the insignificance of his attainment, becomes such as to constitute, in a mind which fairly faces it, a shock to our rational nature sufficient to destroy belief in the rationality of things, and to imperil confidence in the authority of Moral Reason as a guide to human life. To those who have once accepted the rationality of things, and most emphatically to those who have once accepted the faith in a personal God, the improbability that a being of such capacity should have been created to be simply the creature of a day, that ' cometh up, and is cut down, like a flower, and never continueth in one stay,' has almost invariably amounted to an absolute impossibility. It is the favourite argument alike of reasoned Philosophy, and of the intensest moral intuition.'[1]

V

Psychic Researchers and Spiritualists have laboured long in weird and wonderful ways in the search for evidence of survival after death. As far back as 1853, Dr. Tafel published at Tübingen a

[1] *The Theory of Good and Evil*, Vol. II, p. 265.

volume in which he claimed to demonstrate the personal immortality of the human soul, from ninety
authenticated cases of ghostly apparitions. This set
a new fashion, and from that time onwards there has
been a plethora of books purporting, by psychical
evidence, to discredit the oft-quoted line anent the
' bourne from which no traveller returns.'

So common has this sort of thing become that Mr.
Haynes is moved to say : ' Outside religious circles
psychical research holds the field of serious inquiry,
and the mantle of St. Thomas Aquinas has fallen
upon Sir Oliver Lodge.'[1] And though Mr. Haynes
does ' not believe that any one to-day is really convinced by the results of psychical research up to
now, without a strong desire to be convinced,' he
gives it as his opinion (not altogether unbiased)
that those who resort to the spiritualist rather
than the priest get a ' better run for their
money.'[2]

Leaving out of account altogether the vapid nonsense that emanates from the intellectual under-
world of Occultists pilloried by Münsterberg,[3] it is
safe to say that much of the so-called psychical
evidence offered for survival after death is utterly
untrustworthy. Professor Barrett, F.R.S., former
President of the Society for Psychical Research, has
pointed out that the testimony of honest and even
careful witnesses requires to be received with
caution, owing to the constant intrusion of two
sources of error—unconscious mal-observation and

[1] *The Belief in Personal Immortality*, p. 148.
[2] *Ibid.*, p. 109.
[3] *Psychology and Social Sanity*, by H. Münsterberg, Chap. iii.

unintentional misdescription. Mr. Hereward Carrington, in his *Personal Experiences in Spiritualism*, has
shown conclusively that a large percentage of the
spiritualistic manifestations investigated by him were
found to be due to fraud and trickery on the part of
mediums.   Even the world-renowned medium
Eusapia Palladino was caught red-handed, not once,
but several times, by Dr. Hodgson and his fellow
investigators at Cambridge, by Professor Münsterberg, by Mr. Carrington and others.

However, after making all due deductions for
errors of observation and description, for fraud and
trickery, and for chance coincidences, there would
seem to be a small residuum of psychical phenomena
not yet adequately accounted for ; and one feels
that Mr. Hereward Carrington is on the right lines
when he pleads for a thoroughly equipped scientific
laboratory to investigate such phenomena under
test conditions.   The reproach levelled at spiritualistic meetings by Sir William Crookes, years ago, in the
Quarterly Journal of Science, has not yet been
removed.   ' In the countless number of recorded
observations I have read,' wrote Sir William, ' there
appear to be few instances of meetings held for the
express purpose of getting the phenomena under
test conditions.'

It is to experimental psychologists that we naturally turn for scientific explanation of psychic
phenomena, and the opinion of Dr. Quackenbos, as
set forth in his interesting book *Body and Spirit*, may
be taken as fairly representative. He says : ' The
writer has never heard a spiritistic medium say anything that was not readily comprehensible on the

theory of thought transference. He has never seen a medium do anything that could not be rationally explained as due to the action of that supersensible psychic force so fully described in the foregoing chapters.'[1] And he comes to the conclusion that ' the proof of immortality is not to be sought for in the vaporings of spiritism.'[2] Those psychologists who, like Münsterberg, do not accept the theory of thought transference, but explain the phenomenon so described as due merely to a development of man's natural aptitude for interpreting ' motivations of the unconscious,' do not, needless to say, entertain super-normal explanations of spiritualistic pheno-mena.

Sir Oliver Lodge is practically alone amongst men of light and leading in basing his faith in a future life on communications purporting to come from ' the beyond.' A careful perusal of his latest book, *Raymond*, only tends to confirm the view that ' mediumistic communications, which pretend to come from beyond the grave, have never shed the slightest light upon this essential problem ; they have not opened up for us any new and enlarged view of the destiny which awaits us.'[3]

Dr. McTaggart sums up the situation from the standpoint of a calm, impartial investigator when he says : ' Any attempt to prove empirically that man could survive death would have to struggle with such an enormous mass of negative evidence that its antecedent improbability would also not be

---

[1] *Body and Spirit*, pp. 277, 278. [2] *Ibid.*, p. 279.
[3] *Future Life in the Light of Ancient Wisdom and Modern Science*, by Louis Elbé, p. 374.

F

small. Investigation may give us more evidence, and evidence incompatible with any theory except that of survival. But at present it seems to me that we have much more chance of proving our immortality by metaphysics than by psychical research.'[1] It is certainly difficult to understand the mentality of a man who abandons the traditional arguments for a life beyond the grave in favour of the incoherencies of trance mediums and 'direct voice chaps.' We have a sure and certain ground for our belief in a hereafter in the deposit of Revealed Truth. But even apart from that, as we have seen, a purely philosophical consideration of the nature of the soul convinces us that the death of the body does not end all, whilst the argument from common consent, the teleological argument, the ethical argument, each has a cogency that is utterly lacking in the communications purporting to come from ' the other side ' *via* ' Feda,' ' Moonstone,' ' Redfeather,' and the other trance personalities of Sir Oliver Lodge's books.

---

[1] *Some Dogmas of Religion*, by Dr. McTaggart, p. 107.

CATHOLIC EXEGESIS

(An Address to the Inaugural Meeting of the Biblical
Congress, Cambridge)

IT is generally recognised that the last twenty
years represent something more than the conventional dawn of a new century. Already a new
spirit, elusive and perplexing, is discernible in life
and literature. It is difficult to describe and impossible to define, but if the thirteenth century
stands out as the golden age of metaphysics, and the
seventeenth as heralding the reign of the physical
sciences, we may perhaps not inaptly describe the
present as a psychological age. No longer is psychology ' the Cinderella of the Sciences,' rather is
she the ' Queen of the Muses.' There is a psychology
not merely of life, but of art, literature and music—
and there is, too, a psychology of Biblical Criticism
which no Biblical scholar can afford to ignore.

The tone of the Biblical Criticism of the last
century was simply that of the general literary
criticism of the period, which has been characterised
thus briefly and tersely by Professor Saintsbury : ' It
has been the mission of the nineteenth century to
prove that everybody's work was written by somebody else, and it will not be the most useless task of
the twentieth to betake itself to more profitable in-
quiries.' Not only is the rising generation inclined

to dismiss the purely destructive critic, but it seems to be making preparations for the Grammarian's Funeral. It has little use for the type of critic who regretted ' that he had not concentrated his life on the dative case.' His epitaph is written :

> So, with the throttling hands of Death at strife,
>   Ground he at grammar ;
> Still, thro' the rattle, parts of speech were rife
>   While he could stammer.

It is felt that, in the main, textual criticism has reached a point beyond which it cannot be pursued with much profit, and the Biblical scholar who insists on prolonging the discussion as to the precise significance of the Greek article is very much in the position of Serjeant Snubbin, whose absorbing interest was a case about ' a pathway leading from some place which nobody ever came from, to some other place which nobody ever went to.' The fact is that the chief difficulties of the New Testament are common to all its versions.

The present century is still young, but already the thread-bare disputes as to the genuineness and authenticity of the sacred books, to say nothing of the interminable wrangle as to their dates, have given place to a more rational controversy as to their meaning. In this psychological age it is interpretation that matters, not the esoteric interpretation which confines itself to such nice and knotty problems as the ' number of the beast,' ' the little horn,' or the ' Holding of the Four Winds,' but the comprehensive interpretation of the sacred books as a whole, and of the character of the Jesus of History. It would seem as though naturalistic exegesis, after moving in a circle for centuries, has got back to the forgotten starting point of useful criticism. I would invite you to consider for a few moments the broad outline of the history of that exegesis which rejected the guidance of the Catholic Church.

The embittered attacks on the credibility of the sacred books by Celsus, Porphyry and Julian the Apostate are interesting only as early examples of a not particularly enlightened form of criticism which obtains only where there is a pronounced bias against religion. The exegesis of which I am speaking may be said to begin with Luther, who substituted the Bible for the Church, thereby adopting what has been aptly described as ' a strategic rather than an abiding position.' This result of his enthronement of the Bible in the seat of authority was twofold. On the one hand it lead to an arid literalism in interpretation, which was destined ere long to bring its upholders into sharp conflict with the dictates of common sense. This excessive literalism is a markedly characteristic feature of post-Reformation exegesis. As an illustration of it I may point to the story of the creation as set forth by Milton, who in majestic lines describes how . . . .

. . . . now half appeared
The tawny lion, pawing to get free
His hinder parts, then springs, as broke from bonds,
And rampant shakes his brindled mane ; . . . .
. . . .
. . . . : the swift stag from underground
Bore up his branching head.

It was exegesis of this kind which was largely responsible for the alleged conflict between science and religion, as Huxley himself acknowledged when the Darwinian controversy was at its height.

On the other hand, the doctrine of private interpretation naturally led to a very free handling of the sacred text, which, in the latter half of the eighteenth century, culminated in the movement known as Biblical Rationalism. A volume might be written on the subsequent battle of books in which German exegetes mercilessly slaughtered one another. Eichhorn, Strauss and Bauer each blazed a new path, but Naturalism, Mythism and the Tendency Theory are now mere pale spectres of their former selves. Next, the study of comparative religion was held to have reduced Christianity to the level of all other religions, and it was fashionable to look for the origins of Christianity in a syncretism from earlier religions. Blissfully unconscious that the comparative method of Pfleiderer has been discredited because, as the *Encyclopædia of Religion and Ethics*[1] points out, it exaggerated the resemblances and ignored the differences between Christian ideas and the myths and legends of other religions, Mr. H. G. Wells has recently given the public a rehash of the cold remnants of Pfleiderer. This may be all very well for the populariser, but the serious scholar is satisfied, if only on psychological grounds, of the uniqueness of Christ and of His claim. The problem of the twentieth century is to account for that uniqueness. The Christological controversy which distracted the fourth century has been revived in its acutest form, and once again Christendom is at the parting of the ways. As a distinguished Cambridge scholar has

[1] Vol. III, p. 582, Col. 2.

pointed out : ' the issue is daily clearer between those who accept Jesus Christ with his supernatural claim and those who, since they are unable to credit the claim, repudiate His leadership.'[1] The battle is between the old exegesis and the new.

By the old exegesis I mean the exegesis of the Catholic Church ; and the occasion is a fitting one on which to consider its nature and its claims upon our acceptance. Starting with the New Testament writings as genuine historic documents, we find set forth therein the characteristic features of Catholicism—the divinity of our Lord and Saviour Jesus Christ, the fact that He Himself established a visible society with a visible head to be our infallible guide in faith and morals. Naturally, then, we turn to this infallible teacher for her verdict on the Scriptures. It was in this spirit that St. Augustine said : ' For my part, I should not believe the Gospel were it not for the authority of the Church.'[2] She has defined once and for all the divine inspiration of the sacred books, drawn up the Canon of the Scriptures, and laid down certain guiding principles with regard to their interpretation. It is of these that I wish to speak. Of a few texts, on account of their dogmatic implications, she has defined the meaning. Thus the Council of Trent has declared authoritatively that Rom. v, 12, has explicit reference to the doctrine of original sin (*Sess.* v., cc. ii, iv), that John iii, 5, sets forth the necessity of Christian baptism (*Sess.* v., c. iv ; *Sess.* vii., de bapt., c., ii), and that St. Matthew's account of the

---

[1] *Civilisation at the Cross-Roads*, by John Neville Figgs, p. 146.
[2] *Against the Epistle of Manichaeus, called Fundamental*, p. 6.

Last Supper (xxvi, 26 ff.) embodies the doctrine of
the real presence of Christ in the Holy Eucharist.
The Vatican Council has defined the meaning of one
passage in St. Matthew's Gospel (xvi, 16 ff.), of
another in the Gospel of St. John (xxi, 15 ff.). The
meaning of a few other texts, though not directly
defined, has been settled by the use made of them
by the Church in her condemnations of heresy.
These dogmatic texts are, as it were, sign-posts at
the cross-roads of history, marking out the highway
of Christian Tradition. For the rest the Church bids
us keep to the analogy of faith : ' seeing that the
same God is the author both of the Sacred Books
and of the doctrine committed to the Church,' says
Leo XIII, ' it is clearly impossible that any teaching
can by legitimate means be extracted from the
former, which shall in any respect be at variance
with the latter.'[1]

But, it is objected, if the hands of Catholic Biblical
scholars are thus tied by their dogmatic beliefs, their
exegesis, since it lacks freedom, must necessarily be
wanting in sincerity, and theirs will be the inevitable
temptation to do violence to the text in order to
harmonise it with their creed. This objection would
have cogency did the Church exalt the Bible as the
only rule of Faith. But she does nothing of the
kind. She maintains that there are two channels of
divine revelation, the Bible and Tradition. She is
under no necessity to find a warrant for her beliefs
in the written word of God. Why should she attempt to distort texts when she can point to the
living voice of tradition ? I am far from denying

[1] *Providentissimus Deus.*

that individual Catholic exegetes have on occasion
strained the meaning of passages of Holy Writ, with
a view to meeting adversaries on their own ground
of the Bible and the Bible only. But obviously this
is not a vice of the Catholic exegetical system. Were
there no reference in the New Testament, say, to
the doctrine of baptismal regeneration, the teaching
of the Church on this point would remain unaffected.
Hers is not the necessity of finding a comprehensive
creed and formularies within the covers of the
Bible.

Still, you may say, Catholic exegetes are ' cribbed,
cabined and confined ' by the interpretations of the
Fathers. From these they dare not depart without
incurring censure. Where then is their freedom ?
And what is the value of an exegesis that is vowed
beforehand to disregard the fruits of modern
scholarship ? There is a wealth of misconception at
the root of this objection. It is assumed that a
ponderous weight of patristic interpretation has
closed the whole Bible to Catholic scholars. How
far this is from being the case may be gauged by
anyone who will take the trouble to read Pope Leo
XIII's simple pronouncement : ' The Holy Fathers,
we say, are of supreme authority whenever they all
interpret in one and the same manner any text of
the Bible, as pertaining to the doctrine of faith or
morals ; for their unanimity clearly evinces that
such interpretation has come down from the Apostles
as a matter of Catholic faith.' What then is the
position ? The sacred text is not, so to speak, in
the grip of a dead hand. For the interpretations of
the Fathers to be supremely authoritative, it must

first be clear that they are not merely voicing their own individual opinions as scholars or churchmen, but giving expression to the mind of the Church. Only when they can be regarded as the mouthpiece of the living Church do their utterances become coercive, and then it is not because this saint, or this scholar, or this bishop has spoken, but because the Church has expressed her mind. Obviously this can happen only when there is a moral unanimity of interpretation on some point of faith or morals.

Is there anything unreasonable in this ruling of the Catholic Church ? We turn to the early Christian writers and ask them how the primitive Church understood this or that passage of Holy Scripture. If they do not agree, we know that the Church has not spoken, and we are free. But if they do agree, on what rational principle can we set aside the unanimous judgment of primitive Christian writers as to the meaning of primitive Christianity ? In any other field of historical research, say, for instance, with regard to the meaning of a Babylonian inscription, such a consensus of opinion would be regarded as decisive.

Has not the Church a right to express her mind ? The right is conceded to her freely enough in the matter of resisting the spurious interpretations put on Scripture by the Gnostics and Manicheans. There she wins the applause of Christendom, but as soon as she touches live issues the right is denied her. A distinguished Anglican prelate once expressed the opinion that the decision of the Council of Nicæa was ' the greatest misfortune that ever befell the Christian world.' This comes as a shock to pious men who themselves have no hesitation in drawing the line at the seventh, instead of the first, Oecumenical Council. If the Church is to be a witness to the faith that is in her, it is difficult to understand on what principle a time-limit is set to her utility. Collective opinion does not lose its value merely because it cannot be labelled primitive, or even medieval. In all ages, ' a collective authority is,' as Père Lagrange expresses it, ' the natural home of common sense.' The weird, the odd and the fantastic have little chance of passing through the fine meshes of the sieve known as the common teaching of the Church. As one looks at the oddities that lie scattered about on the scrap-heap of nineteenth-century Biblical Criticism, it is impossible not to be impressed with the value of collective opinion as a check on the vagaries of individual minds.

From a purely human standpoint, the Catholic Church has many claims to be heard as an exponent of Sacred Scripture.

She has, in the first place, the necessary psychological qualifications for interpreting them. To understand any classical author properly it is necessary to make oneself acquainted with what is technically termed collateral matter. Anything that will throw light upon the manners and customs of the time at which the author lived is regarded as a valuable addition to the general critical apparatus. What is all this study of ' collateral ' but a painstaking attempt to get into sympathy with the mental outlook of the author and his times ? It cannot be denied that the Catholic Church is in full psychological accord with the New Testament writers.   Their outlook is wholly supernatural, so, too, is hers.   They write of the invisible workings of divine grace, of miraculous interventions in the order of nature, of angels and of devils—and all these things are vivid realities to the Catholic Church.   She lives in the same spiritual atmosphere in which they wrote.   If in an age of ' progress ' this be held against her as a reproach, let it at least be conceded as entitling her to tell us what these early Christian writers really meant.

But more than that.   Not only is she one in spirit with those who wrote the New Testament, she is also one in the same corporate body.   Back through the archway of the ages she traces her apostolic succession, asserting her right by divine inheritance to expound authoritatively the written word of God. No one can contend with any show of reason that the Catholic Church has at any period of her long history notoriously broken with her own past, broken up in the way that dynasties and empires have come to an end to be succeeded by an entirely new order of things.   I would ask you to consider for a moment the exegetical value of this corporate continuity. When in the study of religions there is question of the interpretation of a text, 'back to the monuments' is the cry.   If in the text there is mention of an ancient feast, and we have the written records of people who actually kept that feast, or actual survival of the rite itself, obviously these records and survivals are monuments of prime importance.   No scholar would close his eyes to the light they throw on the text.   If, then, we would understand the gospel account of the last supper, sound exegesis bids us look for enlightenment to that society which throughout the centuries has celebrated the rite of the Holy Eucharist. If to-day, when there is question of the meaning of an ancient Parsee custom or document, scholars eagerly turn to the modern Parsees of Bombay, rightly regarding them as a living monument and commentary on the ancient text, why should we not, in any perplexity as to the meaning of a passage in the New Testament, turn first and foremost to the living monument of the Church of Christ, one in spirit and body with the society of His founding ? Because, it may be answered, in the course of the ages she has corrupted His doctrine and introduced superstitious practices. Now history shows that, whilst all great religious movements are born in a cataclysm, the ideas begotten of the upheaval speedily crystallise, and thenceforth the dominant tendencies of the newly formed community are towards conservatism. The would-be innovator has to face a world in revolt, and such revolts leave their mark in history. I think it must be confessed that the heralds of revolt against the ' innovations ' of the Catholic Church are comparatively few and far between, prior to the disruption of Christendom in the sixteenth century. To-day the charge levelled at the Church is rather that of stagnation than of innovation. She is notoriously conservative, but this very conservatism enhances her value as a living Christian monument.

Finally, it is urged, her claim to be the Church of the Bible disqualifies her as its interpreter. She is an interested party. She cannot be expected to search the Scriptures in a spirit of scholarly detachment.   To which I answer, has any Biblical critic of any shade of belief or disbelief ever approached the study of the New Testament in a spirit of complete detachment ? He has not, for the simple reason that human nature being what it is, it is impossible to do so.   This is a psychological fact which up to the present has not been sufficiently taken into account in estimating the value of exegetical judgment.   As the *Encyclopædia of Religion and Ethics* points out : ' The question of the necessity of approaching the Gospels as historical witnesses with some sort of presuppositions in favour of, or against their testimony, has not yet been treated in a serious scientific manner.'[1] The tremendous issues raised by the New Testament are live issues vitally affecting character and conduct.   No man can read its pages unmoved. Whether he be conscious of it or not, in his daily life he must give practical answer to the question, What think ye of Christ ? It is futile to talk of approaching the study of the scripture as one approaches the study of Homer.   We may fall under the sway of the words of the great Greek poet, but they do not imperiously challenge our daily lives.   When it comes to the interpretation of the New Testament there is no man living who is not an interested party.   Not for nothing did that eminent authority on the study of religion, Professor Jastrow, utter a warning against scholars ' filled with a decided prejudice against religion, which disqualifies them from judging religious phenomena calmly and dispassionately.'[2]

[1] *Encyclopædia of Religion and Ethics*, Vol. IV, p. 320.
[2] *The Study of Religion*, by Morris Jastrow, p. 181.

Precisely because of the temperamental bias inherent in each one of us we have need of authoritative guidance, and therefore a divine guidance has been vouchsafed to us. If the teaching of Christ is to have permanent value in its applicability to the ever-changing problems of succeeding ages, the enthronement of the Church in the seat of authority would seem to be the obvious sequel to a revelation from on high. But even those who reject the Church's claim to divine assistance must yet confess that, in her guidance of Scripture studies, she has shown a sanity which one looks for in vain in the new exegetical methods of that German liberalism which has dominated non-Catholic Biblical Criticism during the past century. Humanly speaking, the Church might have given her official sanction to the allegorical method of interpretation of Origen and the Alexandrian school—it would at least have afforded an easy way in difficult places—but she did not. She might again have hastily revolutionised her methods at the bidding of the New Learning and given the world a *Novum Organon* of Biblical interpretation—but she did not. Always she has steered a middle course between dangerous extremes ; and this same wise policy has recently been set forth by the late Supreme Pontiff, Pius X. Is there anything reactionary in the principles which he lays down ? Listen to his words : ' As we must condemn the rashness of those who, more docile to the seductions of novelty than to the teaching of the Church, do not hesitate to indulge in excessive freedom in the matter of biblical criticism, it is likewise incumbent upon us to disapprove of the attitude of those who do not dare to break in any way with current views in regard to the meaning of the Scriptures, even when, faith remaining unaffected, the wise progress of studies imperiously invites them to do so.'[1]

Nova et vetera—from Origen to Augustine, from Augustine to Jerome, from Jerome to Aquinas, from Aquinas to the humblest of her Biblical scholars to-day, ever out of the abundance of her riches the Church produces exegetical treasures old and new.

[1] Letter to Bishop Le Camus, Jan. 11th, 1906.

RATIONALIST CRITICISM OF THE INCARNATION

(A Lecture to the Cambridge Summer School of Catholic Studies, July, 1925)

RATIONALIST is a very elastic word. It has a great variety of meanings, both as a title of honour and as a term of abuse, and it has the peculiar distinction of having, at least once, completely reversed its signification. In the history of philosophy we find it used originally in connection with Cartesianism, to designate the intellectualist as opposed to the sensist, who sought to reduce all knowledge to sensation; and later, in opposition to the empiricist, who regarded experience as the sole basis of knowledge. The philosophical rationalist stood for the primacy of the faculty of reason over all forms of experience. But, in some strange way, rationalist has come to connote a man who gives not only a primacy, but a supremacy, to experience. Thus an ancient and honourable word has, so to speak, gone over to the enemy. The *Memorandum of the Rationalist Press Association* declares that rationalism 'aims at establishing a system of philosophy and ethics verifiable by experience,' thereby making a speedy end of all

metaphysics, and fulfilling the prophetic words of
Alexander Pope :

> Philosophy, that leaned on heaven before,
> Sinks to her second cause, and is no more.

Certainly empiricism is the basis of the rationalism
which utters the religious challenge. A rationalist in
this sense is defined by Mr. J. M. Robertson as ' one
who rejects the claims of " revelation," the idea of a
personal God, the belief in personal immortality, and
in general the conceptions logically accruing to the
practices of prayer and worship.'[1] In other words,
the out-and-out rationalist is what used to be called
an atheist, but, through a mysterious process of
verbal refinement, has come to be known as an
agnostic.

But rationalist is a term of wider connotation than
agnostic.   In these days it is freely applied to
Modernist divines, apparently without much resent-
ment on their part.   In fact, a writer in the July
Literary Guide (p. 127) tersely defines Modernism as
' rationalism with a theological varnish ' ; whilst, in
the same organ of free thought for October 1924,
Mr. William Archer, commenting on the Oxford
Conference of Modern Churchmen, held last summer
under the presidency of Dean Inge, says :

' What can we do to express our sense of the
Dean's services ? Offer him the chairmanship of the
Rationalist Press Association ? I fear his acceptance
of such a post might offend some of his clerical
brethren—perhaps even his bishop—and one would
be sorry to see him fall out with his caste.   He does

[1] *Rationalism*, p. 4.

much better service within the Church than he could do from outside ' (p. 179).

This, doubtless, is only Mr. Archer's fun, but there are dour and sour rationalists who complain bitterly that the Modernists have stolen their thunder. Certainly there is a great deal in common between the professed rationalist and the ultra-liberal theologian. Huxley said of agnosticism that it was not a creed but a method, and the same is true of rationalism. It is the method of approach to religious questions which really distinguishes the rationalist, whether he be atheist or liberal thinker. Many years ago Lord Balfour pointed out that the vice of method at the root of all naturalism is ' the assumption that the kind of '' experience '' which gave us natural science was the sole basis of knowledge.'[1] The rationalist method is simplicity itself. It is the method of the physical sciences applied out of its proper sphere ; it is ' the probe of chemic test ' imported into the realm of the transcendental. The term rationalist, in this connection, like the term free thinker, is in itself a *petitio principii*. Just as the latter term carries with it the subtle suggestion that nobody else's thought is free, so, too, the former term implies that those who are not rationalists are unreasonable ; presumably that they are in the grip of bigotry, ignorance or superstitition.

The real question at issue, however, is, what precisely is a reasonable criterion of truth in the field of religious enquiry ? Are we justified in summoning everything that claims to be religious truth to the

[1] *The Foundations of Belief*, p. 182, 8th edition.

bar of human understanding ? Must we forthwith rule out of court everything that transcends experience ? Does the world of sense limit the horizon of thought, or may we not rather say thus with Hegel ?

' The rise of thought beyond the world of sense, its passage from the finite to the infinite, the leap into the super-sensible which it takes when it snaps asunder the links of the chain of sense, all this transition is thought and nothing but thought. Say there must be no such passage, and you say there is to be no thinking ; and in sooth animals make no such transition. They never get further than sensation and the perception of the senses, and in consequence they have no religion.'[1]

One of the fallacies enumerated in inductive logic is to look for a kind of proof of which the matter under investigation is not susceptible, demanding greater precision than is attainable from the very nature of the case ; and some such undue delimitation of knowledge appears to be the fundamental fallacy of the rationalist approach to Christology.

Rationalism has scant positive achievement to its credit. Its work is destructive rather than constructive. It is essentially a system of negation and denial, which traces its ancestry back to the philosophical criticism of Kant. For the philosopher of Königsberg, religion was a matter of moral consciousness, and nothing more ; and consequently from the time of Kant onwards a new element enters into Christology, as indeed, in some measure, into every other religious question. Gradually the supreme

[1] *Logic*, Wallace's trans., pp. 87, 88.

test of religious truth became more and more subjective, till we reach the modern introspective
method of the inner approach, according to which
every article of the Christian creed is to be translated
into terms of personal consciousness, and accepted
only in so far as it finds a warrant in that consciousness.

Man has become the measure of all things in a new
sense ; he is the measure even of divinity. Of old the
Arians, though they denied real deity to Christ,
admitted that He proceeded in some extrinsic way
from the Father ; the Sabellians regarded Him as a
glorious, though transient, manifestation of the God-
head ; to the Monarchians even, there was in Him
a spark of the divine, either as a mortal in whom
dwelt the spirit of God, or as a celestial spirit, who
had assumed a human body. But to the Kantian
Modernist, He is at best an individual human
consciousness at its highest.

Whilst the idealistic element in the philosophy of
Kant thus led to sheer subjectivism in religion, the
realistic element of his teaching has an equally
pernicious effect. For his criticism led logically
enough to a sceptical theory of knowledge which,
from the outset, confined itself mainly, if not wholly,
to religious knowledge. It is a theory of knowledge
which ends in doubt, instead of certitude ; a theory
of knowledge which limits the power of knowing
possessed by the human mind to the sphere of sense-
experience, which latter thus becomes the sole test
of reality and truth. Huxley gave an impetus to
the movement in England, and the liberalising
spirit was already rife in Germany. The one and only
text of this new religion is, ' no man hath seen God at

any time.' To talk of the divine, therefore, is to go beyond the evidence, and proclaim oneself execrably unscientific. Hence Christ must be studied as a man, and judged by the standards applied to men. At this stage rationalists vied with each other in paying tribute to Christ. There were those who belauded Him as the dominant, outstanding figure in all history, whose name, as Emerson has it, is not merely written, but ploughed into the story of the human race. Others, again, extolled the depth and the clarity of His practical philosophy, till its absolute transcendence became such a stumbling-block to their naturalistic view of Christ that they found it necessary to take refuge in the fantastic supposition that Christ, during the thirty years of His alleged hidden life, prior to His ministry, must have visited the East and sat at the feet of Oriental sages. So much does the wisdom of Christ transcend the wisdom of the worldly wise. Others again place Christ's uniqueness in His ethical teaching. He is hailed as the great apostle of the brotherhood of man by those who have rejected the fatherhood of God. Indeed, of late years it has become increasingly fashionable to speak and to write of Christ as though His whole message were comprised in the eight beatitudes. These naturalistic views of Christ all ignore His oft-repeated and emphatic claim to divinity, on the tacit supposition that such a claim is preposterous, and must therefore be relegated to the realm of ' mysticism ' which, for the rationalist, is the shadowy abode of poetic fantasy, where Kant's antinomies, or any other impossibilities or contradictories, may dwell in harmony.

So far the general tendency amongst rationalists was to extol the character of Christ, whilst denying His divinity. Thus we were told that, though Christ was mistaken as to His divine sonship, no one could convince Him of sin ; His teaching, too, though considered to be erroneous in the light of rationalist learning, was nevertheless held to find justification in what it had done for the advancement of civilisation. Even Huxley at times seemed to subscribe to the dictum of Bacon : ' There was never found in any age of the world either philosophy, or sect, or religion, or law, or discipline, which did so highly exalt the good of the community, and increase private and particular good, as the holy Christian faith.'

But with the advent of Nietzsche (1844–1900), a new element enters into popular rationalism. So far from admitting anything beneficent in the teachings of Christ, Nietzsche arraigns Christianity as *the* great crime against the human race. In the final chapter of *Der Antichrist* he writes :

' I condemn Christianity. I bring against it the most terrible of accusations that ever an accuser put into words. It is to me the greatest of all imaginable corruptions . . . it has left nothing untouched by its depravity. It has made a worthlessness out of every value, a lie out of every truth, a sin out of everything straightforward, healthy and honest. Let anyone dare to speak to me of its humanitarian blessings ! To do away with pain and woe is contrary to its principles. It lives by pain and woe : it has created pain and woe in order to perpetuate itself.'

The invective of Nietzsche against what he called
the slave-morality of Christianity opened up the way
for assaults on the character of Christ Himself. So
far from being in any sense divine, it was now contended that, even as a man, He was not beyond
reproach. There were blots in His moral character,
else why did He curse the barren fig-tree, when it was
not the season for figs ? Why, too, did He give way
to temper in casting out the buyers and sellers from
the temple ? And how explain His conduct in the
affair of the Gadarene swine ? These exegetical
objections are mentioned, not because they are
difficult, but because they are typical. They need
not detain us long. The malediction of the fig-tree
is obviously symbolical of the fate of Judaism.
Though it was not the season for figs, the abundant
foliage gave promise that the tree might be bearing
fruit even somewhat out of season. So, too, was it
with Judaism, with its extravagant profession and
barren achievement ; and its end was like unto that
of the fig-tree. The anger displayed by Christ in the
temple was not on His own account, because of any
personal pique, but because of His zeal for the house
of the Lord. As He stood in the midst of that scene
of irreverence bordering on sacrilege, His impersonal
anger was the appropriate expression of perfect
holiness. The case of the Gadarene swine is doubtless inexplicable to anyone who closes his eyes to the
proofs of Christ's divinity, even though that be the
one hypothesis that will account for many puzzling
incidents recorded in the New Testament. To one
who accepts the fact that Christ gave permission to
the legion of devils to enter into the herd of swine,

the exercise of His right of soveregin dominion ought
to present little difficulty.

Again, on the intellectual side, it is urged that
there are obvious limitations to Christ's knowledge.
He had to ask the sisters of Lazarus where they had
buried him and, a matter of greater moment, He
was mistaken in thinking that the end of the world
was rapidly approaching ; for, did He not say,
' Amen, I say to you, there are some of them that
stand here that shall not taste death till they see the
Son of Man coming in His kingdom ' (Matt. xvi, 28) ?
However, since Christ elsewhere in St. Matthew
(xxiv, 36) declares with regard to the consummation
of the world, ' of that day and hour no one knoweth,
no, not the angels of heaven, but the Father alone,'
the former passage cannot well be held to refer to
the second coming. With such good reason is it
generally referred to the destruction of Jerusalem,
that rationalist critics are now disposed to make
light of Christ's alleged blunder. Thus, says
Johannes Weiss : ' This solitary limitation of His
discernment, regarding His second coming, is not
worthy of any consideration beside so many proofs
of His perfect knowledge.'[1] The question put to the
sisters of Lazarus raises no difficulty for anyone who
realises that Christ, though truly God, was in habit
found as a man, and that consequently He added to
His store of acquired knowledge through the human
method of eliciting information by questioning.

But there is another and a larger school of rationalist critics which is not concerned about isolated
incidents in the gospels which seem to militate

[1] *Das älteste Evangelium*, p. 87.

against the consubstantiality of Christ with the
Father.   This school takes the New Testament as a
whole, and insists that, if it is studied intelligently,
it reveals the progressive development of the doctrine
of the Incarnation.   Primitive Christianity, we are
told, is one thing, Pauline and Johannine accretions
quite another ;   and it is in these latter that the
origins of the divinity of Christ are to be sought.
This theory of development is usually exhibited in
three stages, in the first of which is presented the
Christ of the Synoptics, then the Christ of Paul, and
finally the Johannine Christ :

(1) The primitive, and therefore the true, picture
of the historic Christ, it is contended, is to be found
in the Synoptics.   Here we have the real man Jesus,
though myth and legend play picturesque parts in
the story of His birth and of His miraculous powers.
The real Jesus of history was the gentle teacher who
walked along the sunlit roads of Galilee or the streets
of Capharnaum with His disciples ;   who discoursed
to the multitude in parables ;   and who was sought
after by little children.   The Synoptics, who knew
Him and loved Him, dwell lingeringly on the intimate details of His life.   So far from claiming
divinity, this Jesus, it is said, even stresses the
distance which intervenes between Himself and God,
as in His answer to the rich young man.   Says Arnold
Meyer : ' When the rich young man addressed Him
with the words, " Good Master," Jesus answered,
" Why callest thou Me good ?   None is good but one,
that is, God."   He has with these words disavowed
bluntly divinity and divine perfection.'[1]

[1] *Was uns Jesus heute ist*, p. 21.

(2) And so, the theory proceeds, the development of Christology proper begins with Paul. He never knew Christ in the flesh and, it is asserted, was plainly not interested in the details of his Master's life. If we are to believe the psychologists who have psycho-analysed Him, Paul was interested in nothing so much as himself. He was a pronounced introvert. The fanaticism of Saul against Christianity, we are assured, is psycho-analytic evidence of his repressed attraction towards the creed of the Nazarene. He was, in fact, torn between two religious complexes, and in the psychic battle which ensued Christianity triumphed over Judaism, and at the crisis, naturally enough, something snapped in Paul's mental mechanism and—the heavens opened, just as they did to Swedenborg and many another unbalanced visionary. The Damascus incident is thus brushed aside by von Hartmann, the originator of the philosophy of the unconscious :

' It was, indeed, no wonder that a notorious visionary and epileptic, in such conflicts of the soul, during a fever in the desert (which was connected with an inflammation of the eyes, and perhaps an inflammation of the brain), was visited by an apparition of the Master of the Church which he was persecuting, as by an objective presentation of the doubts of his own conscience.'[1]

It would be of interest to ask this writer, to what precise period he refers St. Paul's ' notoriety ' as a ' visionary and epileptic.' Nowadays, certainly, we may suppose his visions well-known ; but it is

[1] *Das Christentum des Neuen Testamentes*, p. 201.

extremely unlikely that he had any (or, if this be preferred, imagined that he had any) before that crucial one upon the way to Damascus. But we cannot allow that St. Paul at any time could rightly be called ' a notorious epileptic ' ; such ' notoriety,' at all events, is confined to a narrow circle of theorists, and lacks all serious historical foundation. So, for that matter, does the ' inflammation of the eyes,' thus roundly asserted, for it is at the best but an uncertain conjecture ; much more so the ' inflammation of the brain,' which is a gratuitous aspersion upon one of the greatest men (upon every count) that the world has ever seen. The ' fever ' in this interesting psychological myth is likewise (shall we say ?) a mere ' objective presentation of the doubts ' of the writer. Alas, even the ' desert ' touch, picturesque in itself and helpful to the theory, is particularly unfortunate ; for many miles south of Damascus the country is well watered and fertile, and formerly, says Luthardt, was much more so.[1]

'It is hard for thee,' says our Lord, ' to kick against the goad' (Acts xxvi, 14). St. Paul, then, had misgivings, which may possibly have increased the fury of his persecution. But are these words a sufficient explanation of the tremendous conviction and the tremendous labours of a lifetime ? Not, surely, in the minds of those who overlay them with so much that is mere conjecture or evident fiction. St. Paul had told the tale to the ' beloved physician,' who deliberately repeats it as history (Acts ix, 1–9) ; he told it also to the Jews in the Temple (Acts xxii, 6–11), and to King Agrippa (Acts xxvi, 12–18), and

[1] *Allgemeine Evangelisch-Lutherische Kirchenzeitung*, p. 396.

mentions it elsewhere. He thought that of a sudden he had been struck blind ; he thought that his companions had heard and seen something also. But set aside these difficulties, and it still remains true that his own vision is relatively insignificant amid the overwhelming mass of evidence for Christ's resurrection that he accumulates in the fifteenth chapter of First Corinthians, to which I shall return. Even this, of course, does not exhaust his knowledge of the historical Christ ; but it does show that he had abundant confirmation of that Damascus vision, and that he understood the historical value of that confirmation—far better, indeed, than his critics.

However, it is further assumed that henceforth Paul was subject to ecstatic visions, and that his epistles are, for the most part, rationalisations of his habitual hallucinations, which were the real mind-stuff from which Paul evolved his concept of Christ, presumably in much the same way as a spider spins its web out of its own substance. Christ, for Paul, we are told, is not a man who was born in a stable ; He is a pre-existent, spiritual being, ' a celestial man,' who merely tabernacled amongst men of ordinary mould. In these epistles of Paul, Christ is etherealised out of all recognition by a progressive evolution which stops short, however, at the threshold of divinity, making of Christ no more than the image or the reflection of God.

(3) The real apotheosis of Christ, it is claimed, is to be found only in the fourth gospel. It is, of course, denied that this gospel is the work of John the Apostle. Despite the weight of extrinsic and intrinsic evidence in his favour, he is ruled out of

court. He is an eye-witness ; he must be got rid of. The author, we are told, was a man of much wider outlook than any apostle ; he was a cosmopolitan, a citizen of the world, and therefore probably a native of Ephesus, the melting-pot of Asia, where Greek and Jew and Gentile met in cultured intercourse. Evidence of the kind of syncretism that went on in philosophical and theological matters is to be found in the opening passage of the fourth gospel, where Christ is called the *Logos*.

Now the *Logos* is a Greek concept which goes back to the pre-Socratic philosopher Heraclitus, who flourished at Ephesus some five hundred years before Christ. To the Greeks, order was so conspicuous in nature that they designated the world *Cosmos*, which means ' order.' The correlative of order is reason of some kind—*Logos*. With Heraclitus, fire is the primary impersonal element from which all else evolved, and he calls it the *Logos* in so far as it is, in his scheme of things, the *rationale* of the world. With Plato, the *Logos* becomes an active intermediary in the formation of the world by a God who is far removed from matter. For Aristotle, too, God is remote and inaccessible, and the *Logos* is the ' energy ' in touch with finite things. The Stoics still further developed and purified the concept of the *Logos*, making of it an operative cosmological principle, apparently endowed with intelligence and consciousness. And finally, at Alexandria, the Jew Philo rounded off the doctrine of the *Logos* by weaving into a more or less harmonious whole the Hellenic, Stoic and Hebrew concepts. This *Logos* of Philo is in God as wisdom, and in the world as reason.

Philo vacillates between regarding the *Logos* as a quality at the head of the hierarchy of divine attributes, and hypostatising it in some such way as the Hebrews personified wisdom in the Old Testament (Wisdom xviii, 15 ; lx, 1, 2).

Now the author of the fourth gospel, it is said, simply applied to the historical Jesus the *Logos* fantasies which were current at Ephesus in his day. Thus, says Schmiedel : ' It ought never to be doubted that he [the author of the fourth gospel] has borrowed the word *Logos* and the ideas associated with it from Philo.'[1] The fourth gospel then, in this view, makes of Christ, not merely a ' celestial man,' a sort of mirror of the divinity, but an actual emanation from the abysmal depths of the divine reason, which sustains all else. In Christ the eternal energising force which pervades the universe, as the source and the basis of being and life, is hypostatised in the flesh.

Such are the main outlines of the evolutionary theory which explains away the doctrine of the Incarnation as a subsequent semi-philosophical development of Christ's simple teaching. Since the theory is admittedly based on the New Testament narrative, we may reasonably claim to examine it in the light of documentary evidence.

(1) For the Synoptics, we are told, Christ was merely a man, a great teacher, at best, the Messiah. Yet St. Luke's story of the childhood of Jesus is steeped in the supernatural. Jesus is conceived of the Holy Ghost, born of a virgin, and called the Son of God. Simeon hails Him as a light to the revelation of the Gentiles and the glory of Israel, and at

---

[1] *Das vierte Evangelium*, p. 118.

the age of twelve He astonishes the doctors in the temple with His wisdom and His answers. We may well ask, what manner of man is this ? It is St. Matthew who records St. Peter's confession, ' Thou art the Christ, the son of the living God ' (Matt. xvi, 16). Of St. Mark's gospel, which is regarded as of paramount importance by rationalists generally, the liberal critic, Wilhelm Bousset, writes : ' this oldest of the Gospels is already written from the standpoint of faith ; for Mark, Jesus is already not only the Messiah of the Jewish people, but the miraculous, eternal son of God, whose glory has illumined this world. And it has been rightly re-marked that in this respect our three Gospels are different from the fourth only in degree.'[1] And that prince of rationalist higher critics, Harnack, says : ' already the Jerusalemite Mark has made of Jesus almost a divine apparition, or has found such a conception already existing.'[2] He even sees in Mark, as in John, ' the dominating intention of revealing the divine sonship of Jesus.'[3] Nor does the incident of the rich young man bear the interpretation put upon it by Arnold Meyer, Loisy and others. The young man addresses Jesus as though He were a rabbi, and Jesus thereupon puts to him a leading question which might very well have elicited from the young man an avowal of his belief in Christ's divinity : ' Why callest thou me good ? None is good but one, that is God.' Neither explicitly nor implicitly does Christ deny that He is God. Only by

---

[1] *Was wissen wir von Jesus ?* p. 30.
[2] *Lukas der Arzt*, p. 86, note.
[3] *Ibid.*, p. 119, note.

doing exegetical violence to the text is it possible to read into it any such denial.

(2) The epistles of St. Paul are admittedly hard to be understood, and for that reason alone they intrigue the psycho-analysts. It has been pointed out that psychology has its *bizarreries* no less than metaphysics, and not the least remarkable of them is the complicating of simple problems by looking for explanations in the depths of the unconscious, when all the time they are staring the psychologist out of countenance. It is true that the epistles of St. Paul are not much concerned with the historical incidents of Christ's life ; but this is not because Paul, all unconsciously, had thrust the hard facts of Christ's everyday life into the hinterland of his mind, lest they should conflict with his subjective concept of the supra-mundane man ; no, but for the exceedingly simple reason that the incidents of Christ's life were already well known to the people whom St. Paul was addressing. Besides, St. Paul's very conscious purpose was to deal with pressing problems of the day, and it is quite remarkable how, in dealing with them, he bases his teaching on the words and deeds of Christ. For instance, he says that he esteemed himself to know nothing but Jesus Christ, and Him crucified (1 Cor. ii, 2), and with ringing challenge he ventures his whole creed, his supposed subjective concept of Christ, his alleged visions and hallucinations, the very souls he had won to Christ, all, on a *fact :* ' if Christ be not risen again, then is our preaching vain, and your faith is also vain ' (1 Cor. xv, 14). The historical Jesus is all-in-all to Paul. Does he not say : ' other foundation no man

H

can lay, but that which is laid, which is Christ Jesus ' ? (I Cor. iii, 11).

Christ, for Paul, is no mere man, however etherealised or celestial, ' for,' says St. Paul, ' in Him were all things created in heaven and on earth, visible and invisible, whether thrones or dominations, or principalities or powers : all things were created by Him and in Him ' (Col. i, 16). The general attitude of Paul towards his Master is plainly set forth by Professor Weiss of Heidelberg, whose exegesis can hardly be suspect of inclining unduly towards orthodoxy. He says : ' For Paul, Jesus Himself is an object, not only of faith, but of religious veneration. For him who begs for " grace and peace " not only " from God our Father," but also " from our Lord Jesus Christ," Christ stands on an equality with God ; . . . the practical piety of Paul and his churches expects from Him (Christ) the same as from God—guidance, help, blessing. It gives to Him not only praise, but also addresses prayers to Him . . . Jesus is for the Apostle not only a Mediator, Leader and Model, but also absolutely the object of his religion.'[1]

If Paul were really an introvert subject to hallucinations, his behaviour when his message is challenged has urgent need of psychological explanation. Not only does he make constant appeal to the fact of the resurrection, but in proof of its reality he points, not to the testimony of his own inner consciousness, or to his mystical experience of the vitalising power of the resurrection, or to any of the mysterious things to which he ought to have pointed,

[1] *Paulus und Jesus*, pp. 3, 72.

had he been true to type ; but, like the merest
Philistine without a single complex, he points bluntly
to the testimony of Cephas and the eleven, and to
some five hundred living witnesses who had, with
their own eyes, seen the risen Christ (1 Cor. xv, 5, 6).
His behaviour is psychologically inexplicable, unless
indeed the psycho-analysts are wrong, and Paul
obstinately kept a sane mind in a fairly sound body.
May it not be, perchance, that it is the psycho-
analysts, and not Paul, who have churned things out
of their own inner consciousness ?

(3) Into the question of the Johannine authorship
of the fourth gospel we cannot enter here. It was
written, as the author tells us himself, to show that
' Jesus is the Christ, the Son of God ' (xx, 31), and
St. Irenaeus adds that, in connection with this main
purpose, it was intended also to refute the Christological heresies of the Cerinthians, Ebionites and
Nicolaites. Consequently, the divinity of Christ is
stressed in the fourth gospel in a more marked way
than in the earlier gospels ; and furthermore, with
a view to meeting the philosophical objections of the
heretics of the day, the doctrine is restated, or rather
stated in a new way. The term *Logos*, as we have
seen, was already well known long before the time
of St. John, and there can be little doubt that it was
used by the early heretics in formulating their views
of Christ. This, amongst other reasons, may account
for St. John's use of it in the prologue to his Gospel.
But that he borrowed the *doctrine* of the *Logos* from
Philo, or the Greeks, cannot be seriously maintained
in face of the evidence. The differences between the
Logos of St. John and earlier doctrines of the *Logos*

leap to the eye. In the first place, the *Logos* of Plato and the Greeks is an abstraction, at most, a divine attribute ; whilst Zeller says of the *Logos* of Philo that it ' floats indistinctly midway between personal and impersonal entity.'[1] For the author of the fourth gospel, the *Logos* is a person of flesh and blood, to whom the Baptist bore testimony.

In the second place, the idea of an incarnation of the *Logos* was beyond the horizon of any Greek philosopher ; and as to Philo, it will suffice to cite the testimony of Ueberweg :

' It was impossible that he should conceive of the *Logos* as incarnated, on account of the impurity of matter in his view . . . and for this reason, if for no other, it was impossible for Philo to go farther and identify the *Logos* with the expected Messias, to which course, nevertheless, he was powerfully moved by the practical and spiritual interest connected with redemption through the Messias.'[2]

In the fourth gospel, on the other hand, the *Logos* was made flesh and dwelt amongst us, till He laid down His life for His friends.

In the third place, the *Logos* of Philo is, in his own simile, a chariot-driver doing the will of his liege-lord, and assuredly there can be no kind of identity, nor even community, of nature between a servant and the mighty God of Abraham, Isaac and Jacob. In essence the *Logos* of Philo is the *Logos* of the Greeks with its outlines little altered—a being immeasurably and incalculably below the pure isolated

---

[1] *Die Philosophie der Griechen*, Vol. III, p. 378, 3rd edition.
[2] *History of Philosophy*, Vol. I, p. 231.

perfection of unapproachable deity. But for John, ' the Word was God,' consubstantial with the Father (x, 30), who glorified Him before the foundation of the world (xvii, 24).

In the prologue of St. John, then, we have a statement of the divinity of Christ, made in a manner occasioned by the development of contemporary philosophical and theological speculation. The prologue, however, is in reality a summary of the main thesis set forth in the gospel which follows, wherein the divinity of the *Logos* shines forth in the sayings and doings of Christ, even as in the Synoptics, and in the witness of St. Paul.

As the study of comparative religion is alleged to have discredited the gospel story of the Virgin Birth, so, it is contended, it has reduced the doctrine of the Incarnation to a shaken creed. Such statements ' date ' ; they are redolent of the days when militant rationalists monopolised and moulded the comparative method to bolster up their own theories. From Pfleiderer onwards, the favourite rationalist device for creating the impression that there is nothing unique about Christianity has always been to exaggerate the resemblances, and ignore the differences, between Christianity and other religions. To take an illustration. Mary, the mother of Jesus, is unhesitatingly identified with the Egyptian goddess, Isis. The identification is supposed to be so obvious that only a hide-bound obscurantist would venture to doubt it. One feels a little impertinent in investigating the facts, but they repay investigation. From Apuleius we know that, before the second century, Isis herself had been identified with Minerva, Venus, Diana, Proserpina, Ceres, Juno, Bellona, Hecate and Rhamnasia ;[1] and seeing that the attributes of all these divinities were predicated indiscriminately of Isis, it is certainly not difficult to discover in her some superficial resemblances to the Queen of Heaven. These are stressed, whilst not a word is said about the differences between Isis and Mary. When we recall that Isis always retains the horns of a heifer as a symbol of her kinship with the beasts of the field from which she evolved, that she was wife to her own brother, and that all manner of excess characterised her worship, the process of identification receives something of a check. So, too, is it with the alleged pagan incarnations. Incarnations, in a wide sense, are assuredly to be found in all the known religions of antiquity, but on examination it will be found that the resemblances to the Christian Incarnation are remote in the extreme.

By incarnation is meant the putting on of flesh, of any kind, by a deity or spirit ; and we may at once dismiss as irrelevant all such incarnations as that of Jupiter consorting with Leda in the form of a swan. Again, primitive peoples, in this matter, present no problem. Sir James Frazer testifies that amongst them real incarnations are not found, and that the alleged incarnations, on investigation, have invariably turned out to be cases of the deification of men or animals.[2] In the Latin and Greek classics, too, many so-called incarnations are in reality nothing of the kind, for not infrequently it is only after some

---

[1] *The Golden Ass*, xi, c. 5.
[2] *Lectures on the Early History of the Kingship*, pp. 132 ff., 279 f. (1905).

earthly hero is deified that a divine origin is assigned
to him, presumably to give plausibility to the
deification. Such was the case with Hercules and
Bacchus, and even with Augustus and Plato.

There is, however, a wide range of literature connected with real incarnations of gods in human
flesh ; but the *Encyclopædia of Religion and Ethics*
testifies that ' the conception of one solitary incarnation of deity is peculiar to Christianity.'[1] In
all other religions there is a multiplicity of shadowy
incarnations, or rather manifestations of divinity, as
in the plurality of incarnate Buddhas, or the myriad
animal forms of gods, ghosts and heroes amongst the
Egyptians. In all this, as in the cases of immortal
gods assuming human form to indulge their passions,
one looks in vain for anything approaching a real
parallel to the hypostatic union of the divine and
human natures in the person of our Lord and
Saviour, Jesus Christ.

In addition to stressing similarities and ignoring
differences, the rationalist method proceeds on the
curious assumption that similarity of religious belief
or practice must always be due to borrowing, and
that, if there has been any interchange between
Christianity and pagan cults, Christianity must be
the borrower. This kind of unwarrantable inference
led Professor Rhys Davids to say of the comparative
method that, ' it will be of worse than no service if
we imagine that likeness is any proof of direct
relationship, that similarity of ideas in different
countries shows that either the one or the other was
necessarily a borrower. . . . It would, of course, be

[1] *N. Söderblom* in Vol. VII, p. 184.

going too far to deny that coincidences of belief are occasionally produced by actual contact of mind with mind ; but it is no more necessary to assume that they always are so, than to assume that chalk cliffs, if there be such, in China, are produced by chalk cliffs in the Downs of Sussex. They have no connection one with another, except that both are the results of similar causes. Yet this manner of reasoning is constantly found, not only through the whole range of the literature of the subject from classical times downwards, but even in the works of the present day.'[1]

Some years have elapsed since these words were written, and nowadays, owing to the protests of M. Cumont[2] and other eminent authorities, evidence is required, not of the similarity, which is obvious, but of the borrowing, which is the point at issue.

Of late years it has been borne in upon rationalist anthropologists that a general resemblance in the fundamental religious beliefs of all peoples is a strong argument in favour of the fact of a primitive revelation. If, indeed, the expectation of a godlike deliverer from evil, of a saviour, in the wide sense of the word, is universal in ancient religions, it is at least not unreasonable to suppose that this world-wide expectation had its basis in an actual promise. Nor do the crudities and absurdities of the saviour-myths militate against this view ; for just as a stream is purest at its source and gathers up defile-ment on its way to the ocean, so, too, in the course

[1] *The Origin and Growth of Religion, as illustrated by some points in the history of Indian Buddhism*, pp. 3, 4.
[2] *Les Religions Orientales*, p. 13.

of long ages, the original revelation became infiltrated with barbaric and degrading notions. The fact of a primitive revelation made or kept after the Fall is the simplest and most satisfactory explanation yet offered of what superficial resemblances are actually found in the creeds of all nations. And it is surely not astonishing that everywhere in the history of religions we catch echoes of the primitive promise of divine redemption.

ST. THOMAS AND ARISTOTLE

(A Lecture to the Cambridge Summer School of Catholic
Studies, August, 1924)

(1) Aristotle and his Philosophy

THE glory that was Greece was waning when
Aristotle first saw the light of day at Stagira in
the year 384 B.C. Half a century had elapsed since
the Golden Age of Pericles ; Sophocles and Euripides
were no more ; but Athens was still the shrine of the
mighty. Amongst the contemporaries of the Stagirite
were Praxiteles, Demosthenes and Xenophon ; and
two centuries had yet to run before the tragic end of
Philopœmen, ' the last of the Greeks,' and the passing of Hellas into a province of the Roman Empire.

For the life of the great philosopher we are dependent on uncritical sources. His earliest biographer,
Dionysius of Halicarnassus, wrote some three
hundred years after the death of Aristotle, and only
a fragment of his account remains. In the main we
must rely on Diogenes Laertius, an entertaining
gossip-monger, who wrote some six centuries after
Aristotle. Fortunately, in the fifth book of his *Lives
of the Philosophers*, amongst much that is useless, he
cites the *Chronicles* of Apollodorus, who wrote about
four hundred years earlier, for the salient facts and
dates of Aristotle's career. He has preserved for us

also Aristotle's will, an illuminating document with regard to the philosopher's character, and he gives us a catalogue of the books which Aristotle left behind him, to the number of one hundred and forty-six.

However, he says later that Aristotle's works ' are in number nearly four hundred, the genuineness of which is undoubted.'[1] Possibly, even probably, by books Diogenes means treatises, and certainly long before the time of Diogenes many works were attributed to Aristotle which were not his. Cicero speaks of ' the incredible sweetness of his diction,'[2] and this certainly does not apply to any of the extant writings of Aristotle. In fact, his lack of literary form is so marked as to have drawn down upon him the stigma of being in this matter thoroughly un-Greek. It must be remembered, however, that our Aristotle consists chiefly of the philosopher's lecture notes, which are not only unpolished and disjointed, but, as Professor Burnet has pointed out, not unnaturally treat many important questions very briefly, whilst elaborating obscure points of lesser moment.[3] Within the last twelve months Professor Jaeger has thrown new light on many dark places in Greek philosophy, and it may well be that his *Aristoteles* will bring about a modification of generally accepted views with regard to the period of Aristotle's literary activity, and his philosophical relationship to Plato. The estimate that only about a quarter of Aristotle's

[1] *Diogenes Laertius : Lives of the Philosophers.* Bohn's Classical Library, p. 193.
[2] *Topica,* I, i–iii.
[3] *Aristotle,* by Professor John Burnet : A paper read at the Meeting of the British Academy, July 2nd, 1924.

writings have come down to us is probably correct ; but the marvel is, not that so little, but that so much of his writings has been preserved, for the story of their preservation is, as we shall see in the second paper, a veritable romance in itself.

His personal history is not without glamour. In lineage, it is said, he was a direct descendant of Æsculapius, and son of the court-physician to Amyntas II, king of Macedonia. Of his childhood nothing is known to us, but at the impressionable age of seventeen he was left an orphan, the heir to no mean fortune and the master of his destinies. Because of his full purse calumniators have depicted him as leading the life of the prodigal. But he came to Athens a stripling lad with a northern accent, alien manners, and the temperament of a bookworm. The only prodigality of which there is any evidence was in purchasing books, which he eagerly devoured, so that Plato, his master, called him ' the reader.' If we are to believe Diogenes, he was something of a fop, notwithstanding his unprepossessing person. His legs, says Diogenes, were very thin, his eyes were small, and he spoke with a lisp ; but he bathed in warm oil, dressed in purple and fine linen, adorned his hands with rings, and was most particular as to how he did his hair.

For twenty years, thirteen of them consecutive, he sat at the feet of Plato in the famous Academy. He has been represented as saddening the declining years of ' the old man eloquent,' by his captious criticism, and Diogenes records how Plato is supposed to have said, ' Aristotle has kicked us off just as chickens do their mother after they have been

hatched.'[1] These stories owe their origin to his
constant polemic against Plato's theory of Ideas.
Throughout his works Aristotle is at pains to stress
the points of disagreement with his former master,
though as a matter of fact the points of agreement
are more numerous and more fundamental, so that it
has been well said that Aristotle is ' the greatest of
all Platonists,'[2] in that he sought to purge and purify
the idealism of Plato. Notwithstanding his constant
polemic, he regarded Plato with reverence and
affection. His attitude is well set forth in the
Nicomachean Ethics, where, regretting the necessity
of differing from Plato, he says : ' Still perhaps it
may appear better, nay, to be our duty where the
safety of the truth is concerned, to upset if need be
even our own theories, especially as we are lovers of
wisdom : for since both are dear to us, we are bound
to prefer the truth.'[3] Here, be it noted, he speaks of
' our own theories,' thereby including himself in the
school of Plato.

In the year 345 B.C. Aristotle left Athens to join
his friend Hermias, the governor of Atarneus,
probably for the purpose of instructing him in
politics. The latter, however, was assassinated, and
Aristotle fled to Mitylene with Pythias, the adopted
daughter of Hermias, whom later he made his wife.
She predeceased him : and we find this touching
reference to her in his will : ' Wherever they bury
me, there I desire that they shall also place the bones
of Pythias ' (p. 186). He had been in Mitylene

---

[1] *Op. cit.*, p. 181.
[2] *A Critical History of Greek Philosophy*, by W. T. Stace,
p. 255.   [3] *Nicomachean Ethics*, trans. by D. P. Chase, I, 6.

about two years when Philip of Macedon invited him to undertake the education of Alexander the Great, then a youth of fifteen. For four years Aristotle lived in the royal palace as tutor to the future conqueror, and for three more years he remained in the Macedonian capital. There are wonderful stories of Alexander's munificence to his guide, philosopher and friend. Pliny narrates how the royal patron of learning, in order to foster the study of animals, placed at the disposal of Aristotle several thousand men employed as gamekeepers, hunters, fishermen and fowlers throughout the royal preserves in Asia and Greece.[1]

Soon after Alexander ascended the throne, Aristotle returned to Athens. But ten years had wrought great changes. Plato was dead, and the mediocre Xenocrates had his chair, and the Academy knew Aristotle no more. He therefore opened a school of his own, known as the Lyceum. As an alien he could not acquire real estate, so he is said to have rented a building near the sacred grove of Apollo Lyceius.[2] Others say that the Lyceum was the most sumptuous of all the gymnasia at Athens, elaborately equipped with lecture-halls, baths and arenas for sport, and that Aristotle was permitted to teach, not in the building itself, but as he walked up and down its shady paths with his pupils. Tradition is unanimous that he did walk about whilst discoursing, and consequently he and his followers came to be known as the Peripatetics. For thirteen years he taught and composed his treatises, until political

[1] *Hist. Nat.* viii. 16.
[2] *Aristotle*, by W. D. Ross, M.A., p. 5.

intriguers drove him from the city.   The death of
Alexander the Great in 322 B.C. was the occasion
for an outburst of anti-Macedonian feeling.   As
the tutor and friend of Alexander, the philosopher
was assailed by the over-zealous patriots, who
trumped up against him a charge of impiety, on
the ground that he had given divine honour to a
mortal in a hymn which he had composed in memory
of his murdered friend Hermias.   Mindful of the
fate of Socrates, he fled from Athens lest, as he said,
the Athenians should sin a second time against
philosophy.[1]   The vindictiveness of his enemies
followed him to his retreat at Chalcis in Euboea.
Exile though he was, they declared his life forfeit.
He was beyond their reach ; but Nature executed the
sentence.   He died within a few months of reaching
Chalcis, at the age of sixty-three, in the same year as
his renowned fellow-exile, Demosthenes.

It is difficult to speak in measured terms of the
achievement of Aristotle.   Of him we may truly say
that he touched nothing which he did not adorn, and
he touched wellnigh everything within the range of
human knowledge.   He gathered up and synthesized
all that was of value in the work of his predecessors.
He is at once the culminating apex of Greek philosophy and the forerunner of science.   In an age of
specialists we can only marvel at the sweep of his
intellect.   He was the best informed man of his day
on every known subject of study, and he himself
widened the curriculum of learning by the addition
of several disciplines of which he was the originator.
Rarely does Aristotle strike a personal note, but he

[1] Ps.-Ammonius, *Aristotelis Vita.*

takes a pardonable pride in having invented logic.
' Of this subject,' he says, ' there has not been a part
cultivated, and a part not, before ; nothing of it has
existed at all, . . . about the art of syllogism we have
received nothing at all from the ancients, but we
have laboured for a long time by the exercise of
investigation.'[1] He brings his logical treatises to a
close by asking the reader to excuse any omissions
in his method, and at the same time, ' to be very
grateful for its discoveries.'[2] How well he laid
the foundations may be gathered from Kant's
verdict on deductive logic : ' Since Aristotle it has
not had to retrace a single step . . . and to the present
day has not been able to make one step in advance.'[3]
His *Rhetoric* lays down principles which have never
been superseded. He is a pioneer in zoology, and his
work on the generation of animals displays a genius
that has scarcely been equalled, much less surpassed,
until comparatively recent times. In a letter to
Ogle, 1882, Darwin wrote : ' From quotations I had
seen I had a high notion of Aristotle's merits, but I
had not the most remote notion what a wonderful
man he was. Linnaeus and Cuvier have been my two
gods, though in very different ways, but they were
mere schoolboys to old Aristotle.'[4] He is, too, the
Father of the History of Philosophy, the first book
of his *Metaphysics* being devoted to a critical
appraisement of the work of previous thinkers.
This book must be our starting-point in study-
ing the philosophy of Aristotle, which cannot

---

[1] *Organon*, literally translated by Octavius Owen, Vol. II,
p. 607 : *Sophistici Elenchi*, 183–184.
[2] *Ibid.* [3] *Kritik, Vorrede*, p. 13.
[4] *Life and Letters of Charles Darwin* (1887), Vol. III, p. 252.

rightly be understood apart from its historical setting.

Greek philosophy begins some six hundred years before Christ on the sunlit shores of the Aegean Sea. In its infancy it comes to Athens, ' the eye of Greece, mother of arts and eloquence,' and there attains maturity. Already past its prime it wanders afield to Alexandria, thence to Rome, to Constantinople, Syria and Persia ; and finally, like a weary traveller, returns to the land of its birth, spent and broken, to perish amidst the classic ruins at the closing of the schools of Athens by Justinian in the sixth century after Christ. We may distinguish three great periods in the history of this philosophy. There is first of all the pre-Socratic period, when the Ionics, the Eleatics, and the Atomists looked outward on the world and grappled with the mighty problem of its origin, groping for ultimate constitutive causes. In the second period, from the Sophists to Aristotle, the Greek mind looks inward on itself, and rises from cosmology to epistemology. It soars ever higher and higher with Socrates and Plato, and reaches its zenith in Aristotle. With his death there sets in a period of decadence, the era of the Stoics, Sceptics and Neo-Platonists.

The philosophers of the first period raised the vital question of the nature of reality, and the clash of opinion is sharpest in the theories of the contemporary thinkers Parmenides and Heracleitus. The former stressed the element of permanence amidst apparently changing phenomena. In reality, he contended, change is an illusion ; there is no such thing ; the only reality is imperishable being which

I

never becomes, but always is. Zeno the Eleatic developed this philosophy of the static, and undertook to show by various mathematical conundrums that time, space and motion are chimæras of the mind, delusory notions which resolve themselves into antinomies. Heracleitus, on the other hand, maintained that change is the only reality, and that permanence is an illusion. For him nothing ' is ' but becoming. Everything, he contended, is in a state of flux, and the world itself is a ceaselessly renewed flame. It was Aristotle who reconciled these conflicting views. and insisted that there is in the world both a static and a dynamic element, that in everything finite there is passivity and activity, the determinable and the determining, potency and act, matter and form. This is the pivotal point of Aristotelianism, the theory of hylomorphism, postulating static and dynamic co-principles of contingent being, which therefore, in the last analysis, is seen to be matter determined and made specific.

Still in the first period of Greek philosophy, Anaxagoras at Athens had risen to a supra-sensuous concept of ultimate reality. He was the first to conceive of mind, intelligence, *nous*, as the background of the changing world. Wherefore Aristotle says of him : ' When one man said, then, that reason was present—as in animals, so throughout nature—as the cause of the world and of all its order, he seemed like a sober man in contrast with the random talk of his predecessors.'[1] But Anaxagoras did not make

[1] *Metaphysica* I, iii, 984 : *The Works of Aristotle*, translated into English under the editorship of J. A. Smith, M.A., and W. D. Ross, M.A., Vol. VIII.

mind the sole ultimate principle ; he held to a
dualism of mind and matter, which moves Aristotle
to say : ' Anaxagoras uses reason as a *deus ex
machina* for the making of the world, and when he is
at a loss to tell for what cause something necessarily
is, then he drags reason in, but in all other cases
ascribes events to anything rather than to reason.'[1]
Nevertheless, Anaxagoras made it possible for
Socrates to formulate his far-reaching doctrine of
concepts, upon which are grounded the Ideas of
Plato, the Forms or Essences of Aristotle, and the
Idealism of Fichte, Schelling and Hegel.

At the beginning of the second period of Greek
philosophy the Sophists had radicated all knowledge
in the changing phenomena of perception. This led
to a philosophy of sheer subjectivism. For since
sense-perception varies in individuals, what is true
for one man may be false for another, and the
Sophists certainly did not flinch at the conclusion
that contradictory propositions may both be true.
It was Socrates' mission to restore a belief in objective
truth, and this he did by pointing out that reason is
the stable element in man, and that consequently
knowledge must be radicated in concepts and not in
sense-perception. It was on this foundation that
Plato built up his theory of Ideas. With Socrates the
concept is something purely mental, but the Platonic
Idea is a great deal more : it is a reality apart from
the mind. Ideas are at the head of the whole
hierarchy of concepts and concrete things. The
Idea is, for Plato, the archetypal essence comprising
not merely concepts, but the objective entities

[1] *Ibid.*, I, iv, 985.

which give rise to concepts. In fact these objective entities are real only in so far as they are participations of the Ideas. The Ideas themselves are substances, spaceless and timeless, immutable and imperishable, universals. Ultimately, according to Aristotle, Plato identified them with the Pythagorean numbers. He even makes them the efficient causes of everything and calls them gods. Here, however, presumably he is indulging in the mythical method so beloved by him. But he certainly hypostatised them and attributed to them an existence independent of the objects of sense. Thus for Plato universals are realities apart from mind and matter, existing in a mythical world of their own.

It is on this point that Aristotle joins issue with Plato. The latter, in Aristotle's eyes, had committed the unforgivable sin of divorcing ideas from reality. It is here especially that Aristotle stresses the vital difference between Plato and himself. Both of them describe ideas as ' kinds ' ($\epsilon i \delta \eta$), universals ; but Plato conceives them as something apart from sensible phenomena, Aristotle as something in these. This is due to a fundamental difference in general method. Plato distrusts the senses almost as completely as Parmenides or Zeno. The intelligent man, says Plato, ought not to occupy himself with the things of sense, but with ideas. Aristotle, on the other hand, champions the validity of the senses in their own proper sphere. Each sense reports truly,[1] and whatever error there may be arises from the subsequent judgment on the sense data. Consequently, the starting-point for Aristotle is the

[1] *De Anima* iii, 3 ; *Metaphysica* iv, 5.

world of sense, the things of experience, *facts*. He is the originator of the scientific method, and all its stages—observation, experiment, hypothesis, verification, and deduction—were known to him.

Bacon in the *Novum Organon* accuses Aristotle of ignoring facts and spinning theories out of his head, as a spider spins its web out of its own substance. Nothing could be further from the truth. Aristotle had a passion for facts. Thus he says : ' Lack of experience diminishes our power of taking a comprehensive view of the admitted facts. Hence those who dwell in intimate association with nature and its phenomena grow more and more able to formulate, as the foundations of their theories, principles such as to admit of a wide and coherent development; while those whom devotion to abstract discussions has rendered unobservant of the facts are too ready to dogmatise on the basis of a few observations.'[1] Again, discussing the parthenogenesis of bees, he says : ' The facts, however, have not yet been sufficiently grasped ; if ever they are, then credit must be given rather to observation than to theories, and to theories only if what they affirm agrees with the observed facts.'[2] Bacon in his strictures on Aristotle was guilty of the very fault which he was condemning. He had taken it for granted that the *a priori* method of the decadent Aristotelians[3] was the

[1] *De Generatione et Corruptione* I, ii, 316 : *The Works of Aristotle*, as above.

[2] *De Generatione Animalium* III, x, 760.

[3] For instance, it is narrated of Cremonini (1552–1631) that he would not look through a telescope for fear of finding that Aristotle's astronomy was wrong. *History of Medieval Philosophy*, by M. De Wulf, trans. by P. Coffey, p. 472.

method of Aristotle himself. There are lapses from the scientific method even in Aristotle, but they are few and far between, considering the age in which he wrote.

He is the first to approach the study of concepts in a scientific spirit. He begins with the facts of experience. Individual substances, or 'first substances,' are the original source of concepts. There is nothing in knowledge that is not ultimately accounted for by the individual existents given in the world of realities. The universal is abstracted from individual things, and is alone the proper object of the understanding. It is abstracted by the active intellect (νοῦς ποιητικός) which strips the sensory image of its individualising characteristics, and thus provides a determinant for the passive intellect (νοῦς παθητικός), where as in the womb of the understanding it is conceived and brought forth. Hence for Aristotle the universal exists in the mind, with a foundation in extra-mental reality. This theory has been called the Ontological Modification of Platonic Realism, since it gives to the universal an ontological reality instead of the mythical reality of Plato. It is the most consistent ideogeny yet devised and an enduring monument to the synthetic genius of Aristotle.

The study of the individual things of sense is the constant preoccupation of Aristotle. The principles of any existent thing are for him its causes (ἀρχαί or αἰτίαι), and they are four in number : the material cause, or the stuff out of which the object is formed ; the efficient cause, or the principle of movement which produces the object ; the formal cause, or that

its specific nature ;
...nsic end for which the
...t that Aristotle rejected
Plato as a superfluity. Of
...tle says : ‘ It is possible that
o.   combine all the kinds of causes.
Th.   ., the principle of movement is the
art an   orkmen, the final cause is the work, the
matter   .: earth and stones, and the plan is
the form.’[1]   However, all four causes need not be
present in their separateness, for Aristotle recognised
that the final cause tends to merge into the formal,
and that the efficient cause also is reducible to the
concept of form.   The material cause alone in no
sense comes under that concept.   Ultimately, then,
we are left with two radically opposed mental
abstractions, primary matter and substantial form,
the fundamental categories of Aristotelian philosophy.   By several different routes, as it were,
Aristotle leads us back to the necessary fusion of
the static and the dynamic in the phenomena of
experience.

It has been said that Aristotle’s concept of cause is
in conflict with the scientific concept which lies at the
root of inductive logic.   For Mill a cause is the
immediate, invariable, unconditional antecedent of
the consequent ; and his inductive methods are so
many different ways of purging the antecedent of
mediacy, variability and irrelevant circumstances.
Induction is concerned with the conditions of
sequence in any cycle of changes, and therefore
leaves out of account both final and formal causes.

[1] *Metaphysica* III, 2.

Partisans of Aristotle have laboured to show that Mill is wrong, whilst many moderns have dismissed Aristotle with contempt. The fact of the matter is that Aristotle and Mill are both right. Their conceptions of cause are diverse, but not contradictory. Mill prescinds altogether from the constitutive principles, or reasons, which Aristotle calls causes. So far from denying them, Mill does not even consider them ; they do not come within the range of his vision. On the other hand, Aristotle recognised the scientific notion of cause, as is clear from his enumeration of *post hoc propter hoc* amongst the fallacies, and from his rudimentary treatment of inductive method in the *Topics*.

In one sense the *Logic* of Aristotle is his greatest achievement. In this field he is at once the pioneer and the master, for he had no previous findings on which to work, and throughout the centuries deductive logic has never risen above its source. The term logic is comparatively modern, not being found before the time of Cicero. ' Analytics ' is Aristotle's own name for the principal logical treatises, which at an early date were gathered together with his other logical treatises under the title *Organon*, since logic was regarded as an instrument regulative of all science rather than as a special department of science. These treatises are six in number : the *Categories*, classifying terms out of syntax ; *On Interpretation*, setting forth the doctrine of propositions ; the *Prior Analytics*, or exposition of the formal aspects of syllogistic reasoning ; the *Posterior Analytics*, which correspond roughly with criteriology, or material logic ; the *Topics*, a dissertation on the grounds of probable reasoning ; and finally, the *Sophistical Refutations*, or treatise on fallacies.

It is now generally admitted that the few additions made to deductive logic since the time of Aristotle are, to say the least, doubtful improvements. There is first of all the fourth figure, said by Averroes to have been added by Galen (A.D. 130–200) to the three figures of syllogism recognised by Aristotle. Mr. Joseph says of it : ' The theory of syllogism has been much darkened by this addition.'[1] And rightly, for the fourth figure ignores the all-important denotation of terms which underlies Aristotle's designation of them as major, minor and middle. Hamilton's quantification of the predicate is a still more doubtful boon. The only other addition of any note is the working out of the rules governing conditional syllogisms. These latter were not considered by Aristotle, for the excellent reason that a conditional syllogism can always be reduced to categorical form. Two thousand years of criticism have wrought no substantial change in the logical doctrine of Aristotle, and there has not been a single addition by moderns which moderns have not challenged.

Bacon in his *Novum Organon* mistook the function of Aristotle's *Organon*. The Father of Modern Science, in denouncing the syllogism as a means of interpreting nature, is under the impression that he is correcting Aristotle, whereas it is abundantly clear that Bacon had misconceived Aristotle's doctrine of syllogism. In expounding it Aristotle himself says : ' The peculiar principles indeed in every science are many, hence it is the province of experience to

[1] *An Introduction to Logic*, by H. W. B. Joseph, p. 235.

deliver the principles of everything ; for instance, I say that astrological experience gives the principles of astrological science, for from phenomena being sufficiently assumed, astrological demonstrations have thus been invented. So also is it in every other art and science.'[1] The *Organon*, then, was not meant to be an instrument of discovery, except in so far as it makes the implicit explicit, the confused clear and the indistinct distinct. It is essentially an instrument for testing the validity of the reasoning which proclaims the discovery. It fulfils much the same function as the proof of a sum in arithmetic. It is generally admitted that much of Bacon's criticism of the syllogism is beside the mark, and it was left for Mill to make it clear that induction itself is concerned with establishing the minor premise of a syllogism.[2] Induction is essentially a process of elimination which derives its logical value from deduction. This was clearly seen and stated by Mill : ' The instrument of Deduction alone is adequate to unravel the complexities proceeding from this source (elimination) ; and the four methods (the five methods are grouped as four by Mill) have little more in their power than to supply premises for, and a verification of, our deductions.'[3]

One might have thought that Aristotle would have been content to study the things of sense which so engrossed him, and have devoted himself wholly,

[1] *Prior Anal.* I, xxx, 2. *Organon*, literally translated by Octavius Owen, Vol. I, p. 153.

[2] X is caused by A or B or C or D.
X is not caused by A or B or C.
Therefore X is caused by D.

[3] *A System of Logic, Ratiocinative and Inductive*, by John Stuart Mill, Book III, x, 3 ; 3rd and 4th edition, p. 289.

for instance, to the science of biology, for which he had at once special predilection and special equipment, or at least have been satisfied to set forth the principles of different sciences in unrelated form. But the truth is that he possessed all the concentration without any of the narrowness of the specialist, and just as his encyclopædic bent of mind led him to systematise all previous Greek speculation, it led him also to form a higher synthesis of all the special sciences. He could not confine himself to the study of this or that particular kind of being, say to the study of animals, or plants, or lines, or numbers, as does the zoologist, the botanist, the geometrician and the mathematician ; he felt that he must address himself precisely to that elusive something in which animals, plants, lines and numbers all agree. The objects of the special sciences, the soul in psychology, the inorganic world in cosmology, the celestial bodies in astronomy, all agree in that they are being, i.e., being as distinct from any particular form of being, being in so far as it is being. By being in this sense is meant simply anything which exists or may exist. Mere mental abstractions, such as genus or species, or ' entities ' which are intrinsically impossible, such as square circles, do not come within the notion of being, actual or potential. Real being undoubtedly exists, and clearly this real undifferentiated being may in itself be the object of study, and the portion of Aristotle's philosophy devoted to that study of real being as such is known by the dread title of *Metaphysics*.

This designation is not of Aristotle's coining. It probably owes its origin to Andronicus of Rhodes who, in his edition of Aristotle's works, published about 50 B.C., placed this portion of Aristotle's philosophy after the treatise on *Physics* under the title τὰ μετὰ τὰ φυσικά, to indicate that this section should either stand after, or be studied after, the *Physics*. The word, however, has come to mean above or beyond physics, i.e., transcending experience, and it has fallen into disrepute owing to the beautiful nonsense which has taken shelter under its supposed shadowy vagueness. Aristotle's own name for this branch of knowledge is ontology, the science of being as being, ἐπιστήμη τοῦ ὄντος ᾗ ὄντος. He also calls it first philosophy, in the sense of a governing philosophy which gives laws to all other sciences, but receives laws from none (*Metaph.* I, 2). His own description of it merits more attention than it generally receives. He says : ' If there is no being apart from the compound existences in nature, physics must be the first science. On the other hand, if there is an immutable being, that being must take precedence of the former, and the corresponding science must be the first, a universal philosophy. The office of this philosophy must be the contemplation of being as such, of its essence and its essential attributes.'[1]

For Aristotle the proper object of the mind, as we have seen, is the abstract or universal, and hence the study of being as being ranks higher in the hierarchy of sciences than the study of any particular form of being. Moreover, it involves the study of the first principles, not only of being, but of knowing. In apprehending being as being, the mind is engaged

[1] *Metaph.* VI, i, 28 (1026a).

with that which is most nearly akin to its own immaterial nature. In God this relationship between the knowing subject and the object known is one of absolute identity. Hence it is not astonishing to find that another of Aristotle's names for metaphysics is theology, the science of God, who for Aristotle is thought of thought, νόησις νοήσεως, pure being which is pure thought.

By these names, ontology, first philosophy, theology, Aristotle indicates the precise scope of this much misunderstood branch of philosophy. For him it is not the playground of idle fancy unfettered by fact ; it is an exact science, the basis of which is as empirical as Herbert Spencer's ' probe of chemic test.' Here, as in his psychology, the starting-point for Aristotle is the realistic principle, *nihil est in intellectu quod non prius fuerit in sensu*—there is nothing in the intellect which was not first in the senses. Though he scale the empyrean of metaphysical speculation, he always has his feet on solid earth. Rising from the groundwork of experience, metaphysics is for Aristotle the science of the first principles of being and knowing, and therefore also the science of God, in whom being and knowing are an absolute unity.

The complete philosophy of Aristotle has been classified in various ways. It has been divided into speculative, practical and poetic philosophy. More usually it had been considered under the five headings of logic, metaphysics, physics, ethics and æsthetics. Professor Ross adopts an eightfold division : logic, philosophy of nature, biology, psychology, metaphysics, ethics, politics, rhetoric,

and poetics.[1] In this paper we are aiming at a
bird's-eye view of Aristotelianism as a whole, with
a closer inspection of its main features. Of the
philosophical doctrine set forth in Aristotle's logic,
physics and metaphysics we have spoken. It
remains to set forth briefly the theme of his ethics
and æsthetics. The Stagirite forestalled Kant as
the apostle of independent morality, that is to say,
of a morality independent of any doctrine of a
future life. Plato's transcendental basis of ethics
was rejected by Aristotle, who preached a gospel of
the earth earthy, yet far enough removed from
modern utilitarianism. His ethical theory is the
outcome of his metaphysical theory. True to the
fundamental categories of his philosophy, he insists
that the chief good for man consists in act as opposed
to potency, i.e., in the prudent exercise of all man's
faculties. The chief good, says Aristotle, is ' a working of the soul in the way of excellence.'[2] Excellence
is of two kinds, intellectual and moral. In treating
of the latter Aristotle advocates the essentially Greek
ideal of ' the mean,' that which is neither too much
nor too little. Sophrosyne—temperance, modera-
tion, balance—was the virtue which distinguished
the Greeks from the Barbarians, and it has been well
described as ' serenity at the core of the storm.'[3] In
advocating the doctrine of ' the mean,' the course of
the prudent and intelligent man, Aristotle is merely
giving expression to the spirit of Hellas. And he
was advocating no easily attainable ideal, as the
aberrations of the Epicureans and Stoics testify.

---

[1] *Aristotle*, p. vii.   [2] *Nichomachean Ethics* i. vii. (1098a)
[3] *Greeks and Barbarians*, by J. A. K. Thomson, p. 109.

Aristotle's æsthetics, or philosophy of art, is likewise the outcome of his metaphysics. Plato banished poets from his republic, but Aristotle's insistence on intrinsic teleology in all things would of itself have saved him from such philistinism. Art is defined by Aristotle as ' a state of mind, conjoined with reason, apt to make.' It is essentially productive, and is considered by Aristotle, more particularly in relation to drama, in the *Poetics*. Of this masterpiece Professor Ross says : ' If nothing of his had been left to us but this tiny fragment—on a subject, too, far removed from his main interests—we should still recognise its author as one of the greatest of analytic thinkers.'[1] As we have seen, the proper object of the understanding is the universal ; and philosophy which studies the universal is at the head of the hierarchy of studies. But art, too, is primarily concerned with the universal. It does not aim at a slavish copy of nature ; it idealises nature. It seeks to realise the universal in the individual. Of photography as contrasted with portrait-painting, Aristotle probably would have said what he says of history as contrasted with poetry—it is less philosophical, and therefore less noble, because its object is the particular as such. Into his masterly analysis of the tragic and the comic we cannot enter here. With his *Poetics* as with his *Ethics* we are concerned only in so far as they bear out and illustrate his general philosophical theory.

It is customary to treat the philosophy of Aristotle, like the philosophy of Plato, as the finished product of his thought. But there can be little doubt that

[1] *Aristotle*, p. 276.

had Aristotle, like Plato, lived to the ripe age of eighty, instead of being cut off at the comparatively young age of sixty-three, his work would have received that final revision which it so manifestly needs. Professor Jaeger distinguishes three periods in the literary output of Aristotle. He does not accept the hitherto current view that Aristotle wrote only whilst teaching at the Lyceum. There are vestiges of writings of an earlier period in which Aristotle shows himself more of a Socratic than a Platonist. In the writings of the second period which we possess Aristotle is throughout a disciple of Plato, though not a Platonist in the technical sense. From the pen of the more mature Aristotle we have but little. But had another twenty years of peaceful life been granted to him, undoubtedly the ambiguities, uncertainties and apparent contradictions discernible up and down his writings, as, for instance, with regard to the nature of the soul, the nature of God, and in parts of his *Physics*, would have been in great measure removed, the rough places made smooth, and possibly he himself would have indicated the precise degree of his indebtedness to Plato and his own special, perfected contribution to the heritage of the ages. Masterpiece though his philosophy undoubtedly is, we owe it to him to remember that it never received the finishing touches of the master mind.

At one time or another Aristotle has been the subject of boundless eulogy and unrestrained abuse. In his own day Theocritus of Chios, in an epigram, pillories Aristotle as 'the empty-headed,' and his philosophy is dismissed by another contemporary as

' sad chattering.'[1] The tide of vituperation reached its highest in and around the Reformation period, when Aristotle, on account of the proud position which he had occupied in the schools since the time of Aquinas, not unnaturally incurred the *odium theologicum.* Luther in his downright way said : ' If Aristotle had not been of flesh, I should not hesitate to affirm him to have been truly a devil.'[2] There are no bounds to the invective of Ramus and others of his school, whilst Nizolius, in a work purporting to expose pseudo-philosophers (A.D. 1553), was not ashamed to liken Aristotle to a cuttlefish escaping in a cloud of ink. Again, the rise of the physical sciences produced a reaction against the Stagirite, who was held responsible for ' the lumber of the schools ' in days of their decadence. From being ' the master of those that know ' he came to be only ' the shadow of a great name.' In our own time we have witnessed the swing of the pendulum, and once again Aristotle is at least counted among the immortals. There are obvious defects in his philosophical system, and these we shall consider in estimating the influence of the Philosopher on Aquinas. But, as Hegel reminded an age which had forgotten its indebtedness to the sage of the Lyceum, ' he penetrated the whole universe of things, and subjected its scattered wealth to intelligence ; and to him the greater number of the philosophical sciences owe their origin and distinction.'[3]

[1] *Diogenes Laërtius : Lives of the Philosophers* (Bohn's Classical Library), pp. 184, 185.
[2] Apud Ueberweg, *History of Philosophy*, Vol. II, p. 17.
[3] *Vorlesungen über die Gesch. der Philos.*, II, 298 (1883).

(2) St. Thomas' Use of Aristotle

As Anselm dominates the eleventh, and Abelard the twelfth, so Thomas Aquinas personifies the thirteenth century in the full meridian of its glory.

Many torches contributed to the intellectual blaze of that lustrous epoch. In the first place the thirteenth century was in no small measure moulded by the crusades, of which, after producing five, it saw the end in 1270. These enterprises, and still more the earlier crusades, linked up the East with the West, and brought about an interchange of thought and learning which enlarged men's vision and quickened the spirit of enquiry. If the crusades did not liberate the holy places, they at least liberated men's minds. Moreover, the constant financial drain led to the splitting up of the estates of the impoverished crusaders and the sale of their land to the Jews, and ultimately to the passing away of feudal serfdom, so that the thirteenth century ushered in a freedom of thought and action unknown to the age of Anselm or Abelard.

A still more powerful factor in the revival of learning was the foundation and consolidation of the Universities, especially at Bologna, Paris and Oxford. Dismissing as legendary the story that this historic University of Cambridge owed its origin to one Cantaber, a dashing Spanish prince who flourished in the age of chivalry, or to the sedate monks of Croyland Abbey in 1110, it would seem that the schools at Cambridge, benefiting by a migration of discontented students from Oxford in

1209,[1] shortly afterwards attained university rank. Abroad, Italy alone, during the first half of the thirteenth century, gave birth to no less than nine universities, whilst Spain, in the early decades of the same century, produced three, including the re- nowned Salamanca. Still in the dawn of the thirteenth century, France was dotted with schools which had as good a claim to rank as universities as many in Italy, and doubtless would have done so but for the towering eminence of Paris. The quest of learning was the time-spirit of the age.

A third cause of the diffusion of knowledge was the rise of the Mendicant Orders, the Dominicans, the Friars Minor, the Carmelites, and the Hermits of St. Augustine. Not only did they labour amongst the people, administering to their spiritual and temporal wants, but they had amongst them from the outset men of wide culture, who soon rivalled the most famous doctors of the Universities. The sons of St. Dominic were the first to set a high standard of studies as part of the religious rule. In common with the Franciscans they had to fight their way in the teeth of opposition into university chairs, and once established there they fought each other. This spirit of emulation led to glorious achievement, and soon these two great orders well- nigh captured the universities, so that Roger Bacon, writing in 1271, says that for forty years the secular clergy had not produced a single treatise in theology, and, in fact, had come to think that they could not know anything unless they had sat for ten

[1] *History of Western Education*, by William Boyd, p. 148.

years or more at the feet of the Dominicans and Franciscans.[1]

But greatest of all the causes of the intellectual ferment in the thirteenth century was the rediscovery of the works of Aristotle. Fiction can hardly furnish a parallel to the strange fate which befell the writings of the Stagirite.[2] To his pupil, Theophrastus, who succeeded him as master of the Lyceum, Aristotle bequeathed his manuscripts. On the death of Theophrastus they passed into the hands of his pupil Neleus, who left them as an heirloom to his family in Troas. They promptly hid the precious manuscripts, lest they should be confiscated for the royal library of the Prince of Pergamus. For a century and a half the crumbling pages lay neglected in a noisome cellar. Here, about a hundred years before Christ, they were discovered by Apellicon, a wealthy collector of books, who had them conveyed back to Athens. But they were not destined to remain long in the city of their birth, for at the fall of Athens in 86 B.C., they were seized by Sulla and brought to Rome. About 70 B.C. Andronicus of Rhodes published a complete edition of Aristotle, and for a time there was a revival of Peripateticism. Naturally, interest was greatest amongst Greek-speaking students, and the pivot of Aristotelianism moved East to Constantinople. Nevertheless, as Zeller and

---

[1] *Opera Quædam hactenus inedita Fr. Rogeri Bacon.* Edited by J. S. Brewer (Longmans, 1859). *Compendium Studii Philosophiæ,* cap. v., p. 428. Bacon had no great opinion of the teaching of the two orders, for he adds : ' Propter quod infinita superbia invasit istos ordines, quod præsumunt docere antequam discant ; et necesse est quod doctrina eorum sit in fine corruptionis ' (p. 429).

[2] Strabo, xiii, 1, 54 : Plutarch, *Vit. Sull.* ch. 26.

others have shown, there are indications that notes, at least, of Aristotle's lectures, probably made by his pupils, were in circulation both before and after the edition of Andronicus. Towards the end of the fifth century, Boethius, ' the last of the Romans ' (480–525 A.D.), translated into Latin some of Aristotle's *Organon*, with Porphyry's *Introduction*, and these logical treatises were, according to Abelard, all that was known of Aristotle in the West in the twelfth century.

Strangely enough, considering the constant inter-communication between the Greek Patriarchs and the Popes, it was not through Constantinople that Aristotle was reintroduced to the West. Here begins a second chapter in the romantic history of Aristotle's works. At Constantinople the Christological controversies which distracted the early Church were particularly acute, and in the fifth century a number of Nestorians and Eutychians deemed it prudent to withdraw to the security of the remote and liberal Edessa, where they established a school and devoted themselves to the task of translating Aristotle into the classical language of that seat of Oriental learning, Syriac. Towards the end of the century, however, the Emperor Zeno, at the instigation of Martyrus, the bishop of Edessa, expelled the heretics from ' the Athens of Syria,' and they fled across the Persian border to Nisibis, where they founded schools of logic and theology, and gradually translated Aristotle into Arabic. It is easy to see how Peripatetic philosophy, cultivated by Nestorians and Eutychians under the protection of Persian kings, came to be looked on as the root of heresy, and

Platonism, by contrast, as the ground work of ortho-doxy. Henceforth for centuries Aristotle was an exile from the Christian West, and this period has been described not inaptly as ' the Flight into Egypt.' For Arabian philosophy is Arabian only in name. It is Greek in essence—Aristotelianism with Oriental modifications ; and some of the greatest names of this period of philosophy, Alfarabi and Avicenna, are those of men who were not of pure Arabian descent. Theirs is the glory of having sheltered Aristotle during his long exile.

They were more than mere translators, these Arabians. Alfarabi (†950) wrote many philosophical treatises, and a formal commentary on Aristotle's *Posterior Analytics*. Avicenna (980–1037) set himself to purge Aristotelianism of the Neo-Platonic elements which had been introduced by Alfarabi and others, though it must be confessed that he himself is not free from the taint of Neo-Platonism. With his death Aristotelianism once more incurred the *odium theologicum*. About A.D. 1100 Algazel declared that Aristotelianism was inimical to the creed of Moham-med. This was the beginning of a religious pogrom against culture which led to the burning of whole libraries. Moslem fanaticism waxed apace under the dynasty of the Almohades, until one of these vandals, through political intrigue, was driven into exile to Spain. Then the leopard changed its spots, and the exiled Caliph became a patron of learning.

The Spanish era of Peripateticism was heralded by Avicebron and reached its climax in Averroes (1126–

1198), who, as Dante has it, ' made the great com-
ment,' and abides with Aristotle among the spirits of
the mighty in the ' meadow of fresh verdure.'[1] Like
the Master, the Commentator died in exile, charged
with impiety. Towards the end of the twelfth century the Spanish Caliph deprived Averroes of his
many honours, and pronounced sentence of banish-
ment against him, for that he had cultivated Greek
philosophy to the prejudice of the Koran and the
faith of Islam. To Averroes, Aristotle was indeed
' the master of those that know '; ' he considers him,'
says Ueberweg, ' as the founders of religions are wont
to be considered, as the man who alone, among all
men, God permitted to reach the highest summit of
perfection.'[2] In his Greater, Lesser and Shorter
Commentaries, Averroes claims to mirror the mind
of the master, to be ' faithful found among the faith-
less, faithful only he.' Yet he, too, is tinged with
the emanational conceptions of the Neo-Platonists,
which blended so well with the anti-Trinitarian
theology of the Mohammedans. At his death in
1198, Christian scholars were ready and eager to
quarry in the newly discovered mine. The complete
works of Aristotle were accessible. It was the age of
John of Salisbury, Bernard Sylvester and Peter the
Lombard. The early decades of the thirteenth century saw Aristotle's *Physics, Metaphysics, De Anima*
and other treatises translated into Latin. But these
translations were from the Arabic, Syriac or Hebrew,
or in some way dependent on these versions, and
there soon resulted a welter of variant readings. It

[1] *Inferno* IV, 109-145.
[2] *History of Philosophy*, Vol. I, p. 415.

is to the credit of St. Thomas that he would have nothing to do with these corrupt texts. He obtained permission for two friars of his order, accomplished hellenists, William of Moerbeke[1] and Henry of Brabant,[2] to translate the whole of Aristotle direct from the Greek, and it was on this Latin-Greek version that Aquinas worked. So faithful was this translation to the original that, as Ueberweg testifies, it may serve as a key to the exact reading of the Greek codices from which it was made.[3]

Altogether Aquinas wrote thirteen works in commentary of Aristotle. Unlike his master, Albert the Great, he adheres closely to the text, and never indulges in long digressions. Again, Albert kept his commentary on Aristotle quite distinct from his theology. The supreme achievement of Aquinas was the blending of philosophy and theology into one harmonious whole. There is no haziness of thought about this synthesis. Both in the *Contra Gentiles* and in the *Summa Theologica* he sets forth clearly the relation between philosophy and theology. In the third chapter of the first book of the *Contra Gentiles* he defines the boundaries of the provinces of reason and revelation and, characteristically enough, he bases the delimitation on a principle of Aristotle which he quotes from Boethius : ' The man of

---

[1] Medieval Chronicles which, however, assign wrong dates : In Chronico Slavicorum apud Lindenbrogium ad annum 1249: In Cronico Susati, quod MS. servat Veneta SS. Joannis et Pauli bibliotheca (1267). Also contemporary testimony of Roger Bacon and Bernard Guidon. *Arch. Litt. u. Kirchengesch. Mitt.*, II, 226.

[2] Testimony of Aventinus : *Annalium Boiorum*, Lipsiae, 1710, I, vii, 9, p. 673.

[3] *History of Philosophy*, Vol. I, p. 150.

education will seek exactness so far in each subject
as the nature of the subject admits.'[1] He then continues : ' Now in those things which we hold about
God there is truth in two ways. For certain things
that are true about God wholly surpass the capability
of human reason, for instance, that God is three in
one : while there are certain things to which even
natural reason can attain, for instance, that God is,
that God is one, and others like these, which even the
philosophers proved demonstratively of God, being
guided by the light of natural reason.'[2] Early in the
Summa he returns to the same theme : ' By natural
reason we can know what belongs to the unity of the
Essence, but not what belongs to the distinction of
the Persons.' And he goes on to say that ' whoever
tries to prove the Trinity of Persons by natural
reason, derogates from Faith in two ways : firstly,
by offending against the dignity of Faith, which
is concerned with things surpassing human reason ;
and secondly, by incurring the ridicule of unbelievers,
who suppose that we stand upon such reasons and
believe upon such grounds.'[3] He stresses the point
that there can be no conflict between the teachings
of reason and revelation, since both ultimately
proceed from the God of eternal truth. St. Thomas
thus excludes the pernicious theory of ' double truth,'
which made it possible for a Christian disciple of
Averroes (Siger of Brabant ?) to say that, though
reason compelled him to hold the essential unity of

---

[1] *Nichomachean Ethics* I. 1094b.
[2] *Summa contra Gentiles*, Dominican translation, Book I,
Ch. iii, pp. 4, 5.
[3] *Summa Theologica*, Dominican translation, I, q. xxxii, a. I ;
second number, p. 59.

the active intellect, he nevertheless firmly held the opposite by faith.[1]

St. Thomas' precise demarcation of the boundaries of natural and revealed religion has been criticised on the ground that it led, logically and naturally, to Deism on the part of those who were not convinced Christians. This criticism overlooks the fact that Aquinas was at pains to show that the God of philosophy is not, like an Olympian deity, ' content to sit aloft and watch the world go round,' but a God ' who made the little and the great, and hath equally care of all.'[2] Furthermore, the distinction was necessitated by the development of natural theology since the days of Anselm, and, as we have seen, the classification is in accord with an Aristotelian principle.

The problem before Aquinas in those days of intellectual upheaval was to reconcile Aristotle's acute penetration of nature as a whole with the doctrines of the Christian revelation. And here we have the clue to the few vital points on which Aquinas definitely broke with Aristotle. Naturally they appertain to theodicy : the nature of God, creation *ex nihilo*, personal immortality. These points of departure merit careful study, as they illustrate Aquinas' characteristic use of Aristotle.

And first as to the nature of God. We have seen that the fundamental categories of Aristotelianism are the potential and the actual, and Aristotle does

---

[1] St. Thomas represents this disciple of Averroes (whom he does not name) as saying : *Per rationem concludo de necessitate, quod intellectus est unus numero ; firmiter tamen teneo oppositum per fidem. De Unitate Intellectus contra Averroistas*, Opusculum XVI, Edit. Rom. ; XXII apud De Maria, *Opuscula Philosophica et Theologica*, Vol. I, p. 491.   [2] *Wisdom* vi, 8.

not hesitate to push them to the logical issue of two ultimate principles ; matter that is nothing but matter, pure potentiality, and form that is nothing but form, pure actuality. Actuality is the end to which every existent thing aspires, and in proportion as potentiality is converted into actuality we ascend the scale of being, at the head of which is sheer unconditioned actuality, devoid of all potentiality, and this is God. Now, unlike Plato's *demiurgus*, this pure form does not act on matter directly, but only indirectly, as that which is supremely desirable. Aristotle says : ' Now that which first imparts motion, does so as a thing that is loved. . . . From a principle, then, of this kind—I mean one that is involved in the assumption of a First Mover—hath depended Heaven and Nature.'[1] Incidentally we may remark that Aristotle seems to have thought that motion of this kind was essentially different from motion by impact. The fact that motion by desire ($\H{o}\rho\epsilon\xi\iota\varsigma$), as Aristotle calls it, admits of a mechanistic explanation has been thought to invalidate the famous argument from motion for the existence of God, elaborated by Aristotle in the eighth book of *Physics*. But if motion be taken in the metaphysical sense of transition from potency to act, we may say with Fr. Joyce that the argument ' is securely based on those fundamental first principles, which no physical discoveries can invalidate.'[2]

But, moot questions apart, what precisely is the Aristotelian principle, the point, as Dante has it,

[1] *Metaphysics*, translated by John H. McMahon (*Aristotle's Works*, Bohn's Classical Library), Book XI, ch. vii, pp. 330, 331. In the Oxford trans. by W. D. Ross, Book XII, ch. vii, 1072b.

[2] *Principles of Natural Theology*, p. 86.

from which heaven and all nature hang ?[1] Aristotle raises the question and answers it with precision. The pure actuality which is God is defined by Aristotle as thought of thought ($\nu\acute{o}\eta\sigma\iota\varsigma$ $\nu o\acute{\eta}\sigma\epsilon\omega\varsigma$).[2] That is to say, God is at once subject and object of thought, and therefore thinks only Himself. In Him no other activity is possible, and in this ceaseless self-contemplation lies the divine pleasure which, says Aristotle, ' is always one, *i.e.* simple.'[3] To think anything other than Himself would be to lower Himself, in fact to abdicate His essential changelessness. And thus the affairs of mice and men are beyond the care and ken of the God of Aristotle.[4] This splendid isolation of the Deity is combated by Aquinas both in the *Contra Gentiles*[5] and in the *Summa*. For Aquinas, as for Aristotle, God is form without matter, pure actuality, absolute perfection ; but He is not merely the remote final cause towards which things move, He is through His knowledge the efficient cause of all else. ' Since God is the cause of things by His knowledge,' says St. Thomas, ' His knowledge is extended as far as His causality extends. As the active power of God extends itself not only to forms, which are the source of universality, but also to matter, . . . the knowledge of God must extend itself to singular things, which are individualised by matter.'[6] After treating of the divine knowledge, St. Thomas proceeds to consider the divine will and

---

[1] *Paradiso* XXVIII, 41. [2] *Metaphysics* XI, 9
[3] *Nichomachean Ethics* VII, 14 ; 1154b.
[4] Such is Averroes' interpretation of *Metaphysics* XI.
[5] Book I, cc. l–liv, lxiii–lxxi.
[6] *Summa Theologica*, Dominican translation, I, q. xiv, a. II ; first number, p. 200.

the providence of God, without which not even a sparrow falleth to the ground, thereby altogether transcending the Aristotelian notion of divinity. For the God who is wrapped in self-contemplation Aquinas substitutes the personal God of Abraham, Isaac and Jacob, the God who ' is nigh unto all them that call upon Him in truth.'[1]

From the consideration of the nature of God we pass to the question of the origin of the world. Though Aristotle criticises the crude dualism of Anaxagoras, the logic of his own system leads to an unresolved quality. Since matter is irreducible to form, we are left with two ultimates : form without admixture of matter, and matter without admixture of form. The eternity of matter, taught both by Aristotle and Averroes, had been combated by the theological doctors of Islam and by the older scholastics. They had attempted to disprove the eternity of matter by reason.

St. Thomas, however, adopts a very different line. Like the Jewish philosopher Maimonides before him, Aquinas contends that it is impossible from reason alone either to prove or to disprove the eternity of matter. Maimonides was a sort of Jewish Aquinas, who set himself to harmonise the teaching of the Old Testament with the philosophy of Aristotle, as known to him through the Arabian versions. Strange to relate, this Jewish rabbi exercised a considerable influence in moulding scholasticism. Albert the Great, Aquinas and Duns Scotus were all in some measure indebted to him. Born at Cordova in 1135, he died at Cairo in 1204. His family were driven into exile

[1] *Ps.* cxliv, 18.

by the religious fanaticism of the Almohades, and later he himself incurred the *odium theologicum* of the Jews for having in their opinion, extolled Aristotle to a level with Moses. In passing we may remark that it is indeed curious how Aristotle, throughout the centuries, has been the stormy petrel of religious controversy, whether Christian, Mohammedan or Jewish. Maimonides wrote many works both in Hebrew and Arabic, but the most famous of them is the *Guide of the Perplexed*, in which he sought *ex professo* to reconcile Jewish theology and Greek philosophy. His double allegiance naturally gave rise to many perplexities. Truth he held to be one and indivisible, and consequently for him there could be no conflict between reason and revelation. Yet Aristotle taught the eternity of matter, and the Bible the temporal origin of the world. To this harassing difficulty Maimonides boldly replied that, were the philosophical arguments for the eternity of matter coercive, it would be necessary to interpret the Mosaic cosmogony metaphorically ; but, he maintained, the philosophical arguments are not coercive, reason alone cannot solve the question, and therefore we must abide by the biblical account of the creation of the world in time. In terms of Aristotelian philosophy Maimonides insisted that the primary matter of the world, as well as its form, was in time produced by God out of nothing, *i.e.*, produced from no previously existing entity of any kind.

It was at this stage that St. Thomas took up the question, and with characteristic thoroughness threshed it out in all its philosophical and theological implications. On the one hand, he maintains that it cannot be proved by demonstration that the world always existed, and he adds : ' Nor are Aristotle's reasons (*Phys.* VIII) simply, but relatively demonstrative ; viz., in order to contradict the reasons of some of the ancients who asserted that the world began to exist in some quite impossible manner. This appears in three ways. Firstly, because, both in *Phys.* VIII and in *De Cælo* I, he premises some opinions, as those of Anaxagoras, Empedocles and Plato, and brings forward reasons to refute them. Secondly, because wherever he speaks of this subject, he quotes the testimony of the ancients, which is not the way of a demonstrator, but of one persuading of what is probable. Thirdly, because he expressly says (*Topic.* I), that there are dialectical problems, about which we have nothing to say from reason, as, *whether the world is eternal.*'[1] In the *Contra Gentiles* St. Thomas devotes seven chapters (XXXI–XXXVII) to showing that it is not necessary for created things to have been from eternity, and to answering the objections of his opponents.

On the other hand, he lays it down that ' by faith alone do we hold, and by no demonstration can it be proved, that the world did not always exist.' ' The reason of this,' he says, ' is that the newness of the world cannot be demonstrated on the part of the world itself. For the principle of demonstration is the essence of a thing. Now everything according to its species is abstracted from *here* and *now ;* whence it is said that universals are everywhere and always.

---

[1] *Summa Theologica*, Dominican translation, I, q. xlvi, a. 1 ; second number, p. 243.

Hence it cannot be demonstrated that man, or heaven, or a stone were not always. Likewise neither can it be demonstrated on the part of the efficient cause, which acts by will. For the will of God cannot be investigated by reason, except as regards those things which God must will of necessity ; and what He wills about creatures is not among these, as was said above (q. xix, a. 3). But the Divine Will can be manifested by revelation, on which faith rests. Hence that the world began to exist is an object of faith, but not of demonstration or science. And it is useful to consider this, lest anyone, presuming to demonstrate what is of faith, should bring forward reasons that are not cogent, so as to give occasion to unbelievers to laugh, thinking that on such grounds we believe things that are of faith.'[1]

The indebtedness of Aquinas to Moses Maimonides in this matter of maintaining the insufficiency of reason to prove or to disprove the eternity of matter has been much exaggerated, and it is undeniable that to the study of the vexed question of the origin of the universe St. Thomas made an entirely original contribution. He showed that the philosophical tenet of the eternity of matter was not, as Maimonides thought, in itself irreconcilable with the dogma of creation *ex nihilo*. Primary matter must, in any event, be a creation of God. Even in the *Summa* there are few more masterly passages than that in which he deals with this most subtle question. He says : ' The ancient philosophers gradually, and as it were, step by step, advanced to the knowledge

[1] *Summa Theologica*, Dominican translation, q. xlvi, a. 2 ; second number, p. 248.

of truth. At first being of grosser mind, they failed
to realise that any beings existed except sensible
bodies. And those among them who admitted
motion, did not consider it except as regards certain
accidents, for instance, in relation to rarefaction and
condensation, by union and separation. And supposing as they did that corporeal substance itself was
uncreated, they assigned certain causes for these
accidental changes, as, for instance, affinity, discord,
intellect, or something of the kind. An advance was
made when they understood that there was a
distinction between the substantial form and matter,
which latter they imagined to be uncreated, and
when they perceived transmutation to take place in
bodies in regard to essential forms, such transmuta-
tions they attributed to certain universal causes,
such as the " oblique circle " (the zodiac), according
to Aristotle (*De Gener.* II), or ideas, according to
Plato. But we must take into consideration that
matter is contracted by its form to a determinate
species, as a substance belonging to a certain species
is contracted by a supervening accident to a determinate mode of being ; for instance, man by
(becoming) white. Each of these opinions, therefore,
considered *being* under some particular aspect, either
as *this* (being) or as *such* (being) ; and so they
assigned particular efficient causes to things. Then
others there were who arose to the consideration of
being as being, and who assigned a cause to things,
not as *these*, or as *such* (beings), but (simply) as
beings. Therefore whatever is the cause of things
considered as beings, must be the cause of things, not
only according as they are *such* by accidental forms,

L

nor according as they are *these* by substantial forms, but also according to all that belongs to their being at all in any way. And thus it is necessary to say that also primary matter is created by the universal cause of things.'[1] This, be it noted, is a philosophical conclusion worked out on the basis of Aristotle's metaphysics, and it is in complete harmony with St. Thomas' other dictum, ' that God is the Creator of the world, so that the world began, is an article of faith.'[2]

But great as was the thirteenth-century controversy as to the eternity of matter, there was a still greater controversy with regard to the human soul, which ended only with the definition of the Fifth Lateran Council in 1512.[3] The fifteenth and sixteenth centuries were distracted by conflicting interpretations of Aristotle's psychology. The Averroists contended that Aristotle had held to a shadowy impersonal immortality, whilst the Alexandrists maintained that, in Aristotle's view, the human soul perished utterly with the body. But these days were not yet. St. Thomas had to face a complicated

---

[1] *Summa Theologica*, Dominican translation, q. xliv, a. 2 ; second number, p. 214.

[2] *Ibid.*, q. xlvi, a. 2 ; second number, p. 247.

[3] *Cum diebus nostris antiquus humani generis hostis nonnullos perniciosissimos errores superseminare et augere sit ausus, de natura praesertim animae rationalis quod mortalis sit, aut unica in cunctis hominibus ; et nonnulli temere philosophantes, secundum saltem philosophiam, verum id esse asseverent ; sancto approbante Concilio damnamus et reprobamus omnes asserentes animam intellectivam mortalem esse, aut unicam in cunctis hominibus, et haec in dubium vertentes : cum illa non solum vere, per se et essentialiter humani corporis forma existat, sicut in can. Clementis Papae V in generali Viennensi concilio edito continetur ; verum et immortalis, et pro corporum quibus infunditur multitudine singulariter multiplicabilis, et multiplicata, et multiplicanda sit.* (Ex Bulla *Apostol. Regim.* Leonis X, in Conc. Lateranens. V. edita, 1512.)

problem in its Christian origins, so to speak. What did Aristotle really teach ? And could his teaching be reconciled with the Christian doctrines of the immortality of the soul and the resurrection of the body ? Aquinas had succeeded in reconciling the eternity of matter with the doctrine of creation. Could he make a similar synthesis of reason and revelation with regard to the human soul ? True to his general principle of activity and passivity, Aristotle distinguishes between the intellect which makes (ὁ ποιῶν),[1] and the intellect which suffers (παθητικός), between what St. Thomas calls the Active and Possible Intellect. For Aristotle, the soul is the form of the body, and on Aristotelian principles it perishes with the body. But above this soul which is the entelechy of the body, there is another soul (ψυχῆς γένος ἕτερον).[2] Its characteristics are thus set forth by Aristotle : it is the most divine part of man (De Part. Anim. IV, 10) ; it comes to man from without (De Gener. Anim. I, 3 ; 736b, 26) ; it is a true substance (De Anima I, 4 ; 408b, 19) ; it is thought, pure intelligence, the principle by which we think (De Anima II, 2 ; 413b, 26), and through it man participates in the divinity (De Anima II, 10 ; 656a, 7).

That Aristotle attributes some kind of immortality to this νοῦς ποιητικός, or active intellect, there can be little doubt. He says of it : it is a substance which was not made to perish (De Anima, I, 4 ; 498b, 19) ; it is the only element of our being that

---

[1] Alexander of Aphrodisias, a Greek commentator of Aristotle in the second century, appears to have been the first to call it ὁ ποιητικός νοῦς.   [2] De Anima II, ii, 10.

can exist apart (*De Anima*, II, 2 ; 403b, 26) ; in its separateness it is immortal and eternal (*De Anima*, III, 5 ; 430a, 221), but we are reminded that it is not the whole soul that is separable, but only mind or reason. Zeller has collected many passages showing that the soul which is the entelechy of the body cannot function apart from the body, and therefore perishes with the body. What then is it that survives ? Apparently only the active intellect, which most modern commentators agree was rightly interpreted by Averroes as being one in all men.[1] Hence the immortality adumbrated by Aristotle cannot be in any sense personal ; it does not permit of any survival of the individual after the break-up of the human compositum. It would be soul-survival without self-consciousness, recollection or even sentience.

Far otherwise St. Thomas. In him the main argument for personal immortality reaches its final perfection, and he bases that argument on Aristotelian principles. In the fourteenth article of his *De Anima*, St. Thomas discusses the question, whether the human soul is immortal. He begins by lodging twenty-one objections against immortality, four of them containing explicit references to Aristotle. But in the *Sed contra* Aristotle is quoted again, thus : ' Besides, the Philosopher says (*De Anima* II, 2) that the intellect is separated as a perpetual entity from the corruptible. But the intellect is part of the soul, as he himself says. Therefore the human soul is

---

[1] St. Thomas is generally conceded to have been correct in asserting that Aristotle did not hold the Possible Intellect to be one in all men.

incorruptible.' In Aquinas's view, then, Aristotle
ought logically to have held the doctrine of personal
immortality. For Aquinas, as for Aristotle, the soul
is the form of the body. Against Plato, Aristotle
had emphasised the unity of the soul in its manifold
activities, and St. Thomas now pushes that doctrine
to its logical conclusion. The human soul is the
principle, not only of sensitive and vegetative life,
which it has in common with plants and the lower
animals, but also of the intellectual activities which
are peculiar to man. These latter are shown to be,
in their very essence, independent of matter, and
therefore of the bodily organism. In the present
state of the soul's actuating the body, and operating
through the body, the bodily organs furnish the
material, the data as it were, for the mind's operations ; but it does not follow that the mind cannot
act unless material be provided in this way. Being
essentially independent of matter in its highest
activities of intellect and will, the human soul has
not within it any principle of corruption, and therefore, after the dissolution of the body, it can continue
in conscious activity. Nevertheless even then it is
the form of the body, with a transcendental relation
to the body, which will be realised again at the
general resurrection. St. Thomas insists on this
point to the extent of stating that when we say,
' O ! St. Peter, pray for us,' we are indulging in
metaphor ;   and that strictly we ought to say,
' O ! Soul of St. Peter, pray for us,' since St. Peter
was, and will be again, soul and body in one being.
Thus the doctrine of human immortality is worked
out on strictly Aristotelian lines. Here it may be

said that Aquinas is more true to Aristotelian principles than Aristotle himself. Admittedly there is great confusion in Aristotle's doctrine of the soul, but as to the functional unity of the soul which is the form of the body there is, and can be, no question ; and herein we have the basis of the metaphysical argument for immortality.

In the apologetical *Contra Gentiles*,[1] St. Thomas advances another argument, and this, too, rests on a principle of Aristotle, on a principle that has come to rank with the axioms of Euclid : ' nature does nothing in vain.'[2] St. Thomas states the argument with his customary lucidity and brevity : ' The natural appetite cannot possibly be frustrated. Now man naturally desires to exist always : . . . Therefore man acquires perpetuity in regard to his soul, which apprehends being simply and for all time.' Thus both the metaphysical and teleological arguments for immortality are derived from the Philosopher, as St. Thomas reverently and lovingly calls Aristotle. The concept of God, eternal creation and personal immortality—these are the fundamental points on which Aquinas departs from Aristotle, whilst building up a consistent theodicy based on the principles of Aristotelianism and the data of revelation.

The age in which Aquinas lived was an age of reconstruction. Many brilliant minds besides his own were working on the synthesis of the new learning and the old creed, and it is in the retrospect rather than at the time that Aquinas dominates. Therewere, too, the inevitable reactionaries who were scandalised at St. Thomas' breach with the traditions of

[1] Book II, ch. lxxix.   [2] *De Anima* III, 9, 6.

the earlier scholasticism. Here the points of departure were many and vital. Of the theory of a plurality of substantial forms, Peckham, writing in St.
Thomas' day, says that it still held the assent of the
whole world.[1] Aquinas assailed it, and vindicated
the unity of the substantial form, making it a central
principle of his whole system. In his formulation and
application of this pregnant doctrine he was debtor to
no man ; it is the outcome of his own penetrating
insight into, and broad grasp of, Peripateticism.
Again, he rejected the current opinion that hylo-
morphic composition was the mark of the creature,
and taught the doctrine of subsisting forms, forms
existing without relation to matter, which in-
dividualise themselves, but which are nevertheless
contingent. In these angelic forms, however, he still
recognises a composition analogous to matter and
form, in refusing to identify in them essence and
existence, as he does in God alone. He rejected, too,
the prevalent notion of spermal powers implanted
in matter by God, in favour of the theory of the
eduction of form from the potency of matter. To
the Augustinian theory of the identity of the soul
with its faculties, he opposed the theory of a real
distinction between them severally and the substance
of which they are the powers, though this cannot be
taken to be in any sense an entitative distinction.
In general outlook he was frankly an intellectualist
in contradistinction to the Augustinians who had
proclaimed the primacy of the will.[2] On these and

[1] *Ehrle*, J. Peckham, etc., p. 178.
[2] This academic question is a totally different one from that
debated between intellectualists and voluntarists of the present
day.

other matters so novel did St. Thomas' teaching seem to the Platonising school which actually held the field, that there is no need of further explanation as to why he should have been mistrusted and even opposed with bitter hostility.

It must be remembered that the complete works of Aristotle came to the West in uncritical versions, accompanied by Moorish commentaries, and by at least two spurious works of far-reaching influence, the Neo-Platonic production entitled *The Theology of Aristotle*,[1] and *The Book of Causes*, which St. Thomas says did not come from Aristotle, but from ' Proclus the Platonist.' The glamour of Aristotle dazzled men's minds. Private interpretation of the Bible in the sixteenth century hardly led to greater excesses than private exposition of Aristotle in the opening decades of the thirteenth century. At Paris, Amalrich taught a pseudo-mystical pantheism, whilst David of Dinant identified God with matter and lapsed into crude materialism. Weird and wild speculation ran riot. A steadying influence of some kind was necessary if mental balance was to be preserved, and we are not astonished to find that in 1210 a provincial council, after condemning Amalrich and David of Dinant, decreed ' that neither the books

---

[1] St. Thomas probably refers to *The Theology of Aristotle* when he writes of having seen 14 books of Aristotle in a language which he did not know (Greek or Arabic), these books not having been as yet translated into Latin. He says : *Huiusmodi autem quaestiones certissime colligi potest Aristotelem solvisse in his libris quos patet eum scripsisse de substantiis separatis, ex his quae dicit in principio 12 Metaphysicæ ; quos etiam libros vidimus numero 14, licet nondum translatos in linguam nostram.* (*De Unitate Intellectus Contra Averroistas*, Opusculum XVI, Edit. Rom. ; XXII apud De Maria, *Opuscula Philosophica et Theologica*, Vol. I, p. 467.)

of Aristotle on natural philosophy, nor commentaries on the same, should be read, whether publicly or privately, at Paris.' In 1215 the prohibition was extended to the *Metaphysics* and the Arabian commentaries, though it was expressly stated that the logical treatises might be used in the University. In 1231, Pope Gregory IX, whilst renewing the condemnation of Aristotle's *Physics*, decided to appoint a Commission to examine and expurgate the works of Aristotle. However, doubtless in consequence of Aristotle's real teaching becoming better known, the Commission never sat. For before 1225, under the patronage of the Emperor Frederic II, new translations from the Arabic had been made by Michael Scot, Herman the German and others, so that students were able to discriminate between the real doctrine of Aristotle and its Arabic, Jewish and Neo-Platonic embellishments. By 1254 the study of Aristotle formed part of the regular curriculum of the University of Paris.

During the second half of the century, it was Aquinas, not Aristotle, who became the storm-centre. To the defenders of the older scholasticism he seemed to have introduced many dangerous novelties. Not only seculars and Franciscans, but even fellow-Dominicans fell foul of him, both at Paris and Oxford. Exception was taken, in particular, to his doctrine of the unity of substantial form, and to his teaching with regard to the angels. At Paris in 1270 an attempt was made to have these views condemned. Happily it failed, but in 1277 the reactionaries succeeded in including amongst a number of obnoxious propositions, chiefly taken from

Averroes, certain doctrines of St. Thomas, which were condemned with the rest. In England, the onslaught on Aquinas was led by a Dominican, Robert Kilwardby, Archbishop of Canterbury, who held firmly to no less than four substantial forms. A few days after the Paris condemnation, the University of Oxford, at the instigation of Kilwardby, condemned a number of theses, some of which embodied Thomistic teaching, and not unnaturally that of the unity of substantial form. But this was the end of Dominican opposition to St. Thomas. Albert the Great's uncompromising championship of his illustrious pupil rallied the great Dominican Order, and in 1278 a general chapter held at Milan formally proclaimed the official teaching of the Order to be that of Aquinas, and thenceforth his name and fame were in the keeping of white-robed advocates of great ability, notably of Giles of Lessines and Ptolemy of Lucca. Kilwardby was succeeded in the See of Canterbury by a Franciscan, John Peckham, who in 1286 renewed his predecessor's condemnation of certain Thomistic theses, and urged upon all a return to the earlier scholasticism of St. Francis and St. Bonaventure.

In reality, however, these local condemnations were of little consequence. They had no biding force outside of Paris and Oxford, and they were powerless to arrest the incoming tide of Thomism. The balance, the symmetry and the sobriety of that marvellous synthesis of philosophy and theology compelled the reasoned assent of unprejudiced thinkers, and continued to mould scholasticism until the dark days of its decadence, when Aquinas was as little honoured as

Aristotle in the twilight of Greek philosophy. This synthesis of philosophy and theology is at once the crowning glory and the characteristic achievement of St. Thomas. Even his master, Albert the Great, had spoken with two voices, and the voice of the philosopher was not always in harmony with the voice of the theologian. Not so Aquinas. He speaks always with one voice, in the clear tones of one whose every utterance is an expression of the unification of knowledge. In the Thomistic fusion of philosophy and theology scholasticism reached its zenith. Its decline dates from the neglect of the synthetic principle. And hence Erdmann and others see the beginning of the disintegration of scholasticism in Scotus, who, in excluding creation and immortality from the scope of natural theology, narrowed the realm of reason and widened the sphere of faith, thus opening up the way for his pupil, William of Ockham, to declare that reason plays no part whatever in establishing the truths of religion. The Thomistic antithesis is reached in Ockham's disciple, Gabriel Biel (1425–1495), who stood for the absolute divorce of reason and revelation, and who merits the mournful title of ' the last of the scholastics.'

And thus we have seen how the intellectual anarchy which attended the re-introduction of Aristotle into the West, gave place, chiefly through the genius of Aquinas, to a golden period of balanced culture. But it was as though the synthetic movement spent itself in this highest product of its energies. Even in the lifetime of Aquinas, disruptive principles were at work. *Facilis descensus Averni.* Thomism suffered the fate of Aristotelianism. With the rise of Humanism its eclipse was complete, and for centuries it passed out of the keeping of living minds. The books in which it was expressed moulded in libraries, like Aristotle's parchments in the cellar of Troas. It is true that Aquinas was ' rediscovered ' before the coming of his Apellicon, but he had his Apellicon none the less in one of the greatest of modern Roman Pontiffs, and we cannot more fittingly bring this paper to a close than by citing the enlightened words in which Pope Leo XIII recalled Christian students to the sane study of Aquinas :

' While, then, We pronounce that every wise saying, no matter who said it, every profitable invention or contrivance, no matter who contrived it, is to be willingly and gratefully taken up, We earnestly exhort you all, Venerable Brethren, for the defence and adornment of the Catholic faith, for the good of society, for the advancement of all sciences, to restore the golden wisdom of St. Thomas and propagate it far and wide to the best of your power. The wisdom of St. Thomas, We say ; for if there be in the scholastic doctors any excessive subtlety of inquiry, any inconsiderate teaching, anything less consistent with the ascertained conclusions of a later generation, in a word, anything in any way improbable, We have no mind to hold that up for the imitation of our age.'[1]

[1] *Aeterni Patris*, Aug. 4th, 1879.

PSYCHO-ANALYSIS IN ITS SCIENTIFIC AND ETHICAL BEARINGS

(A Lecture to the Incorporated Secretaries' Association, Liverpool Centre, December, 1932)

OF late years, psycho-analysis, or, the new psychology, as it is sometimes called, has acquired a somewhat unenviable notoriety. It has been exploited by quacks and charlatans, just as hypnosis was when first it came to the knowledge of the general public. It has been written up, and written down, in the daily Press, and, at the present moment, it is a tea-table topic in society. Naturally, it has suffered from this vulgarisation. On the one hand, extravagant and fantastic claims have been put forward by its too ardent supporters, while, on the other hand, it has been ignorantly assailed by writers who are obviously unacquainted with the rudiments of psychology.

However that may be, psycho-analysis in itself has acquired a position of undeniable importance. It is no longer a matter that interests only the professional psychologist. For good or for evil, it is used by the pathologist, the neurologist, the educationalist, the ethnologist, the criminologist, and a host of other -ists, with the result that it calls for careful examination from the moralist.

I propose, first of all, to consider briefly the theory and method of psycho-analysis. It is admitted on all hands that the difficulty of giving a popular account of psycho-analysis is enormous, since one has to grapple with new technical terms, many of them founded on metaphor and mythology, and also with old psychological terms used in an entirely new significance. I shall avoid the use of these technical terms as far as possible, and endeavour to render them intelligible where I have recourse to them.

THE UNCONSCIOUS

Broadly speaking, we may classify our mental states into awareness, consciousness and unconsciousness. I am aware of the things of which I am, at this moment, directly cognisant—the fact of your presence in the hall, and my presence on the platform. I am conscious of a great many things of which I am not immediately aware. I need only advert to these things to see that I am conscious of them ; that it is a Wednesday, that it is the 7th December. But there are a great many things of which I was once conscious, and of which I am now altogether unconscious. These things can only be brought to consciousness with considerable effort or even with the aid of external stimuli. Suppose, for instance, that I have forgotten the name of a certain fountain pen, and try in vain to recall it, I then visualise the poster which advertises it, and see a large white bird carrying a pen in its beak. The bird is a swan and I then remember the name of the pen.

A glance at an old diary for the year 1907 will recall to memory, things which I had, as we say, entirely forgotten. I find an entry in the diary to the effect that in that year I first saw the Cathedral of Milan. I then visualise the Cathedral and the person with whom I visited it, and by this method of association I am able to recall the whole of a long-forgotten conversation. I am able to bring up into the conscious mind things which were previously hidden deep in the unconscious.

Man has been likened by the psycho-analyst to an iceberg, only one-eighth of which is visible ; seven-eighths of it remain submerged, altogether hidden from view, and constituting the real danger of the iceberg. The one-eighth of the iceberg that is visible corresponds with the consciousness of man, the invisible seven-eighths with his unconsciousness. Or, again, man has been likened to the ocean. We can only see the surface or penetrate a comparatively little way beneath the surface. This corresponds with man's consciousness. We cannot see the bed of the ocean and the blind monsters which live, move, and have their being there. The bed of the ocean corresponds with our unconsciousness with its blind instincts and tendencies at work. Psycho-analysis is concerned with the exploration of the unconscious.

Now it is contended, that everything that ever entered consciousness remains. In the course of long years it may be buried deep down in the unconscious, but there it is, requiring only the right association to bring it to the surface of consciousness. For instance, it is said that our instinctive likes and dislikes really go back to the period when we were babies in the cradle. As a grown man, now, you see a person for the first time and you instinctively like or dislike him. According to the psycho-analytic school, the reason is that when you were a baby in the cradle, someone of that type pleased you or annoyed you. And whenever the type reappears, the feeling of pleasure or annoyance associated with it spontaneously rises to the surface. This leads me to explain what is meant by a simplex and a complex.

A COMPLEX

A *simplex* is an idea which has simply its proper connotation. A *complex* is an idea with an undue emotion attached to it. For instance, a window for most of us is something that lets light and fresh air into the room. If, however, as a child you had been held out of a window by a nurse who threatened to drop you if you were not good, for the rest of your life there would be associated with the idea of window the emotion of fear. And this emotion would remain long after the incident which gave rise to it. You would grow up with a phobia, an un-reasoning fear of windows.

There are, of course, many such phobias, and it is contended that most of us suffer from at least one or two. Some people have an unreasoning fear of heights, others of the dark, others of being alone in a closed room, others of an open space, and so on. The psycho-analyst contends that all these phobias are traceable to some long-forgotten incident buried deep in the unconscious. But he goes very much further than that. He contends that if the long-forgotten incident can be dug up and brought to the patient's consciousness, so that he remembers and recognises the incident, he will then be cured of the phobia, or at least can cure himself of it ; just as if you are lying awake at night and hear a noise in the room, it keeps you awake as long as you do not know what it is ; but, as soon as you know the cause of the noise, say the wind moving the blind, your mind is at rest and you go to sleep. To know the cause is to find the cure. And this process of ascertaining the cause is called *catharsis* from the Greek καθαίρειν (to purify). It is the purification of the complex so that it becomes a simplex. Now, *catharsis* is, you will notice, the exact opposite of hypnosis. Hypnosis consists essentially in giving suggestions from without to the patient while he is unconscious. The method of psycho-analysis consists in avoiding giving suggestions to the patient ; but, while he is fully conscious, enabling him, by associations, to trace back some neurosis or phobia to its lair in the unconscious, enabling the patient to revive forgotten memories, and so consciously to fight his inimical complexes.

THE NEW NANCY SCHOOL

Both the psycho-analytic school and the New Nancy school are, in theory at all events, opposed to hypnosis as an essential part of their system. But there, it seems to me, the agreement between the two schools ends. Baudouin, it is true, in his well-known work, *Suggestion and Auto-suggestion*, pays

M

occasional tribute to the psycho-analytic method, but, as the *British Psychological Journal* says : ' His occasional attempts to link up his doctrine with that of psycho-analysis, are not conspicuously successful.' As an illustration of his attempt at reconciliation, I may cite the following passage : ' For cases in which the morbid symptoms are due to spontaneous suggestion by a simple idea, psycho-analytic treatment can never compete in rapidity of cure with suggestive treatment, for the latter (as we have seen) may give instant relief. But where the trouble is due to spontaneous suggestion by complex, psychoanalytic treatment, though tedious, may save time in the end, and may give more satisfactory results. If I may use the similitude, psycho-analytic treatment is to suggestive treatment what algebra is to arithmetic. It complicates simple problems, but it simplifies complex problems ' (p. 240).

If I understand Baudouin aright, his contention is that a pernicious suggestion may be radicated in a complex. This suggestion has to be uprooted, and according to the New Nancy school, it can be uprooted only by counter-suggestion, which, since it purifies the complex, may be regarded as a form of *catharsis*.

Manifestly this process is, in one important respect, the exact opposite of *catharsis*, which above all is a conscious process. One can only regret that Baudouin did not take his courage in both hands, and bring the two schools face to face, for clearly, *catharsis* is not suggestion, and suggestion is not *catharsis*. Each, as a therapeutic method, has much to its credit, but it is futile to pretend that they are fundamentally the same. It is undeniable that the aim of psycho-analysis is to bring into the full consciousness many of the dark things which the New Nancy school would leave for ever buried deep in the depths of the unconscious.

MOTIVATIONS OF THE UNCONSCIOUS

However that may be, it is evident that feelings and emotions which are stored up in the unconscious are continually manifesting themselves in spite of us. This they do in so-called chance actions, slips of the tongue, mistakes in reading and writing, absent-minded actions, and so on. These chance actions are described in the language of psycho-analysis as motivations of the unconscious. The unconscious, we are told, expresses itself in spite of us, and gives away our real judgments about men and things. Byron hit upon this truth when he wrote : ' constant thought will overflow in words unconsciously.' Let us take a few illustrations. An amusing instance is recorded by Brill. A certain American citizen, who was notorious for his meanness, invited a number of friends to spend an evening at his house. As the evening wore on, instead of giving his guests supper, he handed round sandwiches and lemonade. Later in the evening one of the guests was discussing President Roosevelt's character with his host, when he said, ' you can say what you like about Roosevelt —but he always gave you a square *meal*.' Of course, he meant to say a square *deal*, but the unconscious asserted itself in spite of him. An instance of the unconscious asserting itself in reading is that of the pessimist who read that the Government had *unfounded* confidence in the Navy, when the printed word before his eyes was *unbounded*. Chance actions are looked on as ' symptomatic,' as indicating our unconscious but, nevertheless, true judgments and feelings about things. So, according to Freud, when the lady of the house breaks things, this is an indication that she is dissatisfied with them. But if the maid breaks them it is because unconsciously, she reacts against cleaning them and consequently gets rid of them.

Briefly then, psycho-analysis may be described as the Science of the unconscious. Perhaps the best formal definition is that of Oskar Pfister : ' psycho-analysis is a scientifically grounded method devoted to neurotic and mentally deranged persons, as well as to normal individuals, which seeks by the collection and interpretation of associations, with the avoidance of suggestion and hypnosis, to investigate and influence the instinctive forces and content of mental life lying below the threshold of consciousness.' According to Pfister, then, it is an investigation of the instinctive forces lurking in the unconscious. But, what are these instinctive forces ? Psychologists, generally, would say that they are reducible to two primitive instincts : the instinct of self-preservation, and the instinct of self-reproduction, both of which are reducible to what is described as the instinct of vital continuity. Now, in the normal life of civilised man, he is not engaged in a constant struggle with his natural enemies to preserve his life. The instinct of self-preservation rarely comes into play,and consequently,it is contended that the other primal instinct, that of self-reproduction, acquires undue prominence. For this reason, Freud and his school radicate practically all the motivations of the unconscious in the sex impulse. Freud is rightly regarded as the father and founder of psycho-analysis, and the psycho-analytic method. Ever since his first publications on the subject, in season and out of season, he has stressed the element of sex. There are, however, to-day, different schools of psycho-analysis, notably the schools which follow Jung and Adler. Though not agreed, they differ from Freud chiefly in their refusal to radicate everything in sex.

Opponents of Freud

According to Adler, who was one of Freud's earliest pupils, sex is a mere appendage of the ego. The most basic instinct is to preserve and assert one-self. He agreed with Nietzsche that the fundamental drive of life is the will to power. And this is true even where sex appears to be dominant. Every nervous crisis is due to some kind of inferiority complex. For instance : there was an English officer who was a complete nervous wreck as a consequence of the blowing to pieces of the men under his command, while he remained uninjured. He had lost his self-esteem. On analysis it was found that when a child he had been weak and sensitive, and that his father had called him ' sentimental Jimmy.' When he recognised that he had been suffering from an inferiority complex he was cured of his habitual nervousness.

Jung formulated a theory more embracing and logical than this. He maintains that Freud's theory applies to one psychological type, and that Adler's theory applies to another. Jung's theory does justice to both types. Sex is one libido, or energy, or urge : self is another. Energy in itself is neither good nor bad. But whenever it is not properly disposed of there will be nervous trouble. There are two well-defined psychological types, namely : the *intravert* and the *extravert*. The intravert uses thought as the function of adaptation—he thinks beforehand. The extravert uses feeling as the function of adaptation—he feels his way to action and thinks afterwards. The intravert feels, but does not show it, except on conventional lines : he is cold and dry, the type of whom people say : ' Still waters run deep.' The extravert thinks, but inside and not as a function related to external life. He is of an impulsive nature. Neurosis, in the case of the intravert, is a conflict between conscious thought and unconscious feeling ; in the case of the extravert it is a conflict between conscious feeling and unconscious thought. Jung points to many striking cases. For instance, an intravert, a business man, retires from business and goes in for social life, to entertain and be entertained. He breaks down in health because he has not developed feeling as the function of adaptation to external life. He was a pronounced intravert, who adapted himself to external reality by thought ; sentiment was kept in the background. When he retired from business, he had at hand a great deal of disposable energy which refused to be disposed of in the conventional forms of feeling. When he felt at all, his feelings were of the physical order, he felt ill and became ill.

It is probably true enough that our primitive instincts are entirely egotistical. Obviously, these have to be repressed if any kind of social order is to be maintained. And in our waking conscious life, they are repressed from infancy onwards by our ideas of refinement, education, religion, civilisation, and other formative factors in our lives. The sum-total of the forces which cause this repression is personified and called the censor.

Now these primitive tendencies, we are told, may be repressed too severely, or in the wrong way, and unless some sublimation be found for them, the result will be a complex issuing in phobias, neurosis, or nervous disorders. ' Hoist with his own petard ' is the psycho-analytic diagnosis of most of man's mental and nervous troubles. The lady who fears that other ladies are talking about her in her absence has usually been a pretty accomplished back-biter herself. The detective not infrequently ends by imagining he is being shadowed, and it has been pointed out that the liar's real punishment is that eventually he is unable to believe that anybody else is telling the truth.

Freud himself tells us that the royal road to the unconscious is the study of dreams ; and, perhaps his most valuable contribution to psychology is his theory of dreams. Stripped of the everlasting sex-obsession of Freud as it has been stripped by Havelock Ellis and others, the theory is certainly of some value.

INTERPRETATION OF DREAMS

Some dreams, especially dreams of children, are quite frankly the fulfilment of conscious wishes. The little boy, who, during the day, has craved for chocolates, not infrequently during the night dreams that he has them and that he is eating them. Where the conscious wish is strong, adults also, occasionally, dream in this undisguised fashion. No Daniel is needed to interpret such dreams.

But what of the ordinary fantastic nonsense that most of us dream every night ? Every such dream, according to Freud, also embodies the fulfilment of a wish, but here the wish has been repressed during the waking life by the censor, and consequently, the fulfilment is in symbolic form. During the day there is a constant check or censorship on all our thoughts, desires and actions. When we sleep, the censorship is in abeyance, and the repressed wish expresses itself not literally, but symbolically. However, it may be objected that terrifying dreams cannot be interpreted as the fulfilment of repressed wishes. For instance, a child dreams that its mother is dead. In this dream, as in every other, according to Freud, we must distinguish the manifest content of the dream, and the latent content. The child is frightened at the manifest content of the dream, the death of its mother. But the latent content is quite different. Death to the child mind is a symbol of separation, and the dream indicates a repressed wish on the part of the child to be separated from, to get away from, its mother for a while. The repressed wish has found an outlet in symbolic form.

Symbols

Some symbols are common to the whole race, others are proper to nations or individuals, but in any case, the symbolism of the dream is due to some recent incident. The unconscious seizes upon that incident, or part of it, and uses it as the vehicle of expression for that which was repressed. During the war I remember a lady telling me that her son Alfred was reported missing. She told me that no less than three different ladies to whom she had spoken of the matter, dreamt that Alfred had returned safe and sound. This, however, did not represent an unselfish wish on the part of those three ladies, that the missing Alfred should return safe and sound. The psycho-analytic explanation is that the missing Alfred became to each of those three ladies, a symbol of someone else who was absent, and who was near and dear to her. In each of the three cases, the dream was the fulfilment of a repressed wish (repressed perhaps because of its impossible nature) that some absent loved one, symbolised by Alfred, should return.

The technique of psycho-analysis resolves itself into various methods of unearthing repressed wishes or inhibited desires, buried deep in the depths of the unconscious. The interpretation of dreams naturally plays a large part in this process.

Word-Association

But there are other ways, the chief being what Jung calls word-association or reaction to test words.

The method is simplicity itself. A number of disconnected words are read out to the patient who, after each one, mentions the first word that comes into his head, no matter how irrelevant or ridiculous the word may appear. Jung has drawn up a list of one hundred test words for which it is claimed that it contains words capable of stimulating nearly every possible emotion. The average reaction time for the majority of persons is 2.4 seconds per word. If the patient exceeds this time, and especially if he very much exceeds it, it is claimed that the word has touched an emotional complex, and it is the duty and business of the analyst to unmask that complex completely, by further test words, free associations or other similar methods. He must be, in Tennyson's phrase, ' keen through wordy snares to track suggestion to her inmost cell.'

The Moral Dangers of Psycho-Analysis

Now psycho-analysts insist that during the treatment, in no case is the patient ever to withhold from the analyst any thought, however intimate or delicate. Bearing in mind the great part that is assigned to sex-impulses by Freud and his school generally, the moral danger of this sort of self-manifestation, especially when it is made to a person of the opposite sex, is obvious. This danger, I think, cannot be stressed too much. At present any charlatan is free to describe himself or herself as a psycho-analyst, and lead others to physical and moral ruin, so that it is not surprising to find even psycho-analysts declaring that the time has come when, in the interests of social sanity, the practice of psycho-analysis ought to be regulated by law.

This is the more necessary when we consider a further stage in the technique of psycho-analysis— the stage known as transference. The analysis takes a very long time—the shortest cases take an hour a day for three months, and some an hour a day for three years. In the course of this analysis, the analyst must seek to draw upon himself the emotional component of the discovered complex. In the words of one of the masters of psycho-analysis, transference is described as ' the displacement on to the physician of various affects (feelings), that really belong to some other person.' This transference of erotic feeling to the physician is regarded as an integral, and even essential, part of the analysis, and I need hardly enlarge upon its moral dangers. They are admitted by the greatest analysts themselves, who even feel it incumbent on them to take precautions against such dangers. Thus, one Harley Street psycho-analyst points out that, while the analyst ' should always be thoroughly understanding and sympathetic, he should carefully refrain from personal intimacy, and more especially from anything in the nature of physical contact.' And he adds : ' Personally, I never even shake hands with my patients till they are cured and leaving me.' The honour of the medical profession is above suspicion, but, unfortunately, psycho-analysis is practised by people who do not belong to the medical or any other profession, and in their hands, the method of transference can only receive the unmitigated condemnation of all right-minded men.

It is true, of course, that transference is not the end of the cure. The affect transferred to the physician is ultimately to be displaced by what is called sublimation, by which process the affect is to be directed into a legitimate channel. It may be sublimated in art, music, intellectual or manual labour. But, before it is so directed, or in case of its not being successfully directed, the moral danger is enormous. At the best, in the hands of a skilled and competent analyst, transference remains a perilous venture, and this even from the purely psychological point of view; in any case it is a venture for which it is certainly difficult to find moral justification.

Now, it is a bold thing to criticise psycho-analysis, because, at once, the psycho-analysts take to analysing the critic and invariably discover in him repressed complexes of a very disreputable character, which have led him to react against the new science.

CRITICISM OF PSYCHO-ANALYSIS FROM STANDPOINT OF ETHICS

However, I venture to say that so far as practical ethics are concerned, what is true in psycho-analysis is not new, and what is new is not true. The earliest Christian teachers understood very well that there is a constant warfare between the ' law of the mind ' and ' the law of the members.' It is no discovery of psycho-analysis that we are prone to evil from our very childhood, and that our evil inclinations must be checked, sublimated, if you prefer the word. Psycho-analysis can claim many dramatic cures, but none quite so dramatic as the way in which the vices of the pagans who were converted to Christianity were sublimated into virtues. The censor is merely a new name for the voice of conscience (the sum total of inhibiting forces). As for transference, is not the whole scheme of Christian ethics directed to transferring our affections from the temporal to the eternal, till we attain to that blessed state in which there are no material wants or appetites at all? The analyst, I am afraid, not infrequently takes upon himself the office of confessor or spiritual director, and that without the aid of grace.

From Standpoint of Psychology

Psycho-analysis has added nothing of any real value to rational psychology. The analyst may reply that his psychology is empiric, and that he has no more concern with rational psychology than with metaphysics. The obvious answer is that if he is to co-ordinate his results and present them in intelligible form, he must have a rational psychology of some sort.

Now, it seems to me, that of all the psychological theories as to the relation of mind and body, none is so convenient to psycho-analysis as the neo-scholastic system of metaphysical monism. Let us briefly glance at the rival theories in the light of psycho-analytic findings.

Epiphenomenalism gives a primacy to matter,

regarding consciousness as a mere aftermath of the brain process. It would appear to be the exact opposite of the psycho-analytic theory. Still less satisfactory is the theory of Interaction which destroys individuality and unity in man, and makes of him a mechanical union of a corpse and a ghost. The motivations of the ghost, however unpleasant, cannot be held to affect the health of the corpse ! Psycho-physical parallelism is useless as an explanation of the causal connection between mind and matter, since it denies any such connection between the physical and the psychic processes.

If the psycho-analyst is to find justification in rational psychology, he must fall back on the scholastic doctrine of the substantial unity of the soul and body. As Cardinal Mercier has pointed out, the new scholasticism ' is in possession both of a systematic body of doctrines and also of an organic framework, quite capable of receiving and assimilating the ever-increasing products of the sciences of observation.'

It seems to me, that in the Aristotelian-Thomistic teaching is to be found a ready-made interpretation of the latest facts in connection with unconscious mental states. It has been remarked by philosophical reformers that Aristotle has a disconcerting knack of turning out to be right after all. He says : ψύχη ἐστὶν ἐντελέχεια ἡ πρώτη σώματος φυσικοῦ δυνάμει ζωὴν ἔχοντος, or as St. Thomas expresses it, ' anima est perfectio prima primusque actus corporis naturalis organis præditi.' Herein lies the key to a satisfactory explanation of man and the solidarity of his acts. Never for an instant does St. Thomas lose sight of the substantial unity of soul and body. He even points out that when we utter the invocation ' O ! St. Peter,' we are merely using a figure of speech, and that philosophically, we ought to say ' O ! Soul of St. Peter,' since his soul is at present separated from his body, whereas St. Peter was, and will be, body and soul in one complete entity. Such being the doctrine of the Scholastics, they were in no danger of neglecting to study the operations of man's animal nature, which they interpreted as proceeding ultimately, from the one vital principle in man, the ψυχή, the soul.

Psycho-Analysis and Scholastic Anthropology

I have said enough, I think, to make clear my point, that there is a natural alliance between the empiricism of the psycho-analysts, and the rational psychology, or if you will, the anthropology, of the Scholastics. Psycho-analysis has at least that much in its favour, and I submit that that alone is sufficient to make us eager to take a hand in its formation. Only too often in the past have we stood aside and allowed a new discovery to be moulded in the interests of materialistic or agnostic philosophy. It was late in the day before rationalists were made to feel that the study of comparative religion was a two-edged weapon. Need we leave it so late before taking the psycho-analytic method out of the hands of the secularists ?

Lord Morley tells a story of a young man who once applied to him for a post on the staff of a leading daily paper. When asked if he had any special qualification the youth replied, ' Yes, invective.' ' In what particular line ? ' asked Morley. ' Oh, no particular line,' said the young man, ' just general invective.' The pity is that so many periodicals seem to retain writers with the gift of general invective. Psycho-analysis has now taken the place of hypnosis as the legitimate object of any amount of abuse. One can only hope that some of these writers will soon have exhausted the adjectival resources of the language and be compelled to desist from want of ammunition. Apparently they are not in the least concerned that whilst they are gathering up the tares they are rooting up also with them, the wheat.

St. Thomas Aquinas did not reject the works of Aristotle, because they came to him from a tainted source, through the hands of the Mohammedan scholars, who had perverted the text with their comments. He fearlessly, in the face of a good deal of opposition, undertook the work of purification. The muddy stream of psycho-analytic literature does, indeed, need purification, but already the purifying operation has begun. A sane psychology must necessarily join issue with psycho-analysis as to the everlasting parading of sex-matters. And it is not only the philosophy that has received Christian baptism which joins issue. When psycho-analysis was in its infancy, a vigorous protest against its so-called truth-talk in relation to sex-matters was made by one of the most distinguished of modern psychologists, who, however, did not hesitate to adopt whatever he found of worth in the psycho-analytic method, and who certainly cannot be accused of prudery. The policy of unveiled speech in regard to sex-matters, adopted by the psycho-analysts, was denounced by Professor Münsterberg as ' the greatest psychological crime of our day.'

EXPLOITATION OF PSYCHO-ANALYSIS

Though the Freudians may be right in seeking a biological basis for their theory, few psychologists will deny that the sex-element has been unnecessarily obtruded on our notice. This has given a handle to unscrupulous popularisers who have exploited psycho-analysis for the purpose of achieving big sales amongst prurient-minded readers. In circulating libraries I have seen, both in London and New York, thrown in the way of the ordinary novel-reading public, books which outrage every canon of decency, and which undoubtedly constitute a very real danger to the community. They are professedly written in the interests of science, though it is obvious in some cases that their authors have not even a nodding acquaintance with the rudiments of normal psychology. Reputable psycho-analysts deplore this sort of thing as much as we do ; but in the meantime these social pests are increasing in number, polluting the minds of the young, and it is high time that something was done to check them. Whatever be the merits of legitimate psycho-analysis, it has certainly become a weapon of offence in the hands of the carnal-minded. Condemnation on this point can hardly be too severe.

N

Much of the criticism directed against psycho-analysis, however, appears to be beside the mark. It is argued, for instance, that it implicitly denies free-will. Now, Freud and many of his disciples are out-and-out determinists, but this is an idiosyncrasy of theirs and by no means essential to psycho-analytic theory, as Dr. Bousfield made clear some years ago. All science is, in one sense, deterministic in its outlook, but this does not involve denial of freedom in man.

Again, it is urged against psycho-analysis that it is dangerous to manifest to a patient the evil propensities lurking within him. Convince a man that he has an unconscious tendency to become a thief, and as likely as not you may make him become one.

To this the analyst replies that, if the patient is so disgusted with his tendency to steal that he has repressed it and thrust it deep down into the depths of the unconscious, he is hardly likely to foster it when it stands revealed in all its naked hideousness. And in any case, we are reminded, it is the business of the psycho-analyst to induce the patient to sublimate the evil tendency.

GENUINE DANGERS

Nevertheless, there is, undoubtedly, weight in the objection. Once the tendency stands revealed, the danger of its coming into action by the power of auto-suggestion is very great. Guyau, in his work on *Education and Heredity*, has pointed out the un-wisdom of revealing to people their evil propensities.

He judiciously remarks that it is extremely
foolish, when a child has done wrong, to express
censure in the form of a generalisation such as,
' what a greedy boy you are ; what a liar ; what a
naughty child.' The child thus characterised, looks
upon itself as a glutton, as a born liar, and so on,
and acts accordingly. It is far better policy, according to Guyau, to show great surprise that so good
a child, one habitually so truthful, should have
lapsed slightly and told a lie to-day.

It would be futile to pretend that psycho-analysis
is a science ; possibly it is the hope of a science, but
it must be confessed that the arbitrary interpretations put upon dreams, chance actions and other
motivations of the unconscious by expert analysts
of the different schools, are calculated to give the
sane man pause.

Again, the attempt to dethrone intellect in favour
of will is altogether unnatural. The emotional drive
to action may be powerful, but experience testifies
that, normally, self-control rests ultimately with the
reasoning faculty. Furthermore, words need not be
wasted on the shallow-minded psycho-analysts, who
proclaim that religion, moral principles, self-
discipline and the great guiding factors of life, are
merely rationalisations. In fact, according to these
pundits, everything, except sheer lawlessness, finds
shelter under that glorious umbrella-word. This is
precisely the kind of thing that has rightly brought
psycho-analysis into contempt. It has suffered
much from those who have exploited it in the
interests of agnosticism.

Psycho-analysis has been tossed about in many a

storm, and the breakers of metaphysics, ethics, psychology and science have well-nigh driven it on to the rocks. As scholastic philosophers, exponents of the *philosophia perennis*, our only interest is to see if we can salvage something from the floating wreckage.

ADVENTURES IN PSYCHOLOGY

I

THERE are some people who seem to think that to have a bad memory is *prima facie* evidence of a keen intelligence, and it is often assumed that if a man has a remarkably good memory he cannot be a really profound thinker.

Nothing could be further from the truth. A really first-class memory is impossible without accurate and systematic thinking of a high order. Memory has been called the Master of the Rolls to the Soul, and that master has no easy task. Reflect, for a moment, on the rate at which impressions are being received by every sense of your body, to be registered ultimately in the vast files of the unconscious.

Is it true that some people are born with bad memories? It is true in the same way that some people are born with bad eyesight or bad hearing, that is to say, the material organs of vision or audition are in some way imperfect. For in memory there are two distinct elements, the one physiological and the other psychological.

1. The physiological element is that of *retention* and depends entirely on the physical quality of the brain. Every sensation that is received by the senses of the body passes along the afferent nerves

to the brain, upon which it literally makes an indelible impression.

Some brains are more plastic than others and receive impressions more clearly and more easily. But in the course of years the best brain becomes covered with a network of ruts, until finally in extreme old age it cannot receive any more. This accounts for the fact that very old people can remember the happenings of their youth, but not the incidents of yesterday. The former events are literally engraven on their brain, whereas the latter are not recorded.

A retentive brain, like a good digestion, is a gift. It is not something that can be cultivated, and since it is a physical quality of the brain itself there is no means of improving one's retentiveness. From this point of view, then, there is no remedy for a bad memory.

2. But, then, there is also in memory a psychological element called *recollection*. It consists in the psychic process of digging something up from the unconscious and bringing it into awareness. Broadly speaking, we may classify our mental states into awareness, consciousness and unconsciousness. I am aware of the things of which I am at the moment directly cognisant, for instance, that I am writing. I am conscious of a great many things of which I am not immediately aware. I need only advert to these things to see that I am conscious of them ; for example, that it is raining, that there is industrial depression in the country.

But there are a great many things of which I was once conscious and of which I am now altogether unconscious. These things can be brought to the surface of consciousness only with considerable effort, and sometimes only with the aid of external stimuli. Suppose that I have forgotten the trade name of a commodity which I wish to purchase. I try in vain to recollect it. I then visualise the poster which advertises the commodity and see the picture of an animal which I recognise, and I then instantly recall the name of the commodity because it has been named after the animal. Recollection, then, is made by way of simple association, the simpler the better, a fact that should be borne in mind by advertisers.

The device of tying a knot in your handkerchief to make you recollect something is a crude instance of the associative method. It is crude, because the knot has no intrinsic connection with its message. It does not point immediately and exclusively to the object to be remembered.

In the bad old days it was thought that the best way to train the memory was by mechanical repetition. The schoolboy kept on saying ' dormire, to sleep ' until he nearly exemplified his words. Nowadays the boy is taught intelligently. He knows what a dormitory is, and he is informed that the word dormitory is derived from the Latin dormire, which means to sleep. The dormitory in which he actually sleeps is the associative link between the Latin and English words to be learnt.

This associative method is the basis of all modern systems of memory-training. As we have seen, you cannot improve your power of physical retention, but you can improve your psychological faculty of recollection. In other words, you can improve your memory by better thinking, by linking up fact with fact, and correlating your experiences into one harmonious whole.

Many people with normal powers of retentiveness have bad memories because of mental laziness. Recollection implies two vital factors, namely, attention and association. Attention, or concentration is the first requirement, and yet it is astonishing how many people are lacking in this fundamental constituent of memory. Some years ago it was my lot to examine many hundreds of scripts written by civil servants in answer to a series of intelligence tests. The first test was for attention, thus :

' Write on the right of this sentence the first of the words which are pronounced alike but spelled differently.'

The number of candidates who wrote either the wrong word, or wrote on the left of the printed sentence, was amazing. After the tests for attention there followed various tests for general intelligence, and these took the form of supplying correlations. As a simple instance, the candidate was asked to supply a word in the following sentence :

' As mountain is to hill, so ocean is to —— .'

The tests are graduated until they involve quite complicated correlations. It will be noted that these tests are again based on the associative method.

Now a man who attends carelessly and allows pieces of information to enter his mind as detached items is not likely to have much power of recollection. On the other hand, the man who concentrates on what is before him and receives every impression in its proper setting, so to speak, has not merely got a good memory, but he has got also the makings of a genius. Genius has been defined as an infinite capacity for taking pains, taking pains, that is, in concentration and association. With him everything that enters consciousness finds its logical place in the apperceptive mass of knowledge, instead of being a detached slab of information. With him every item of knowledge is in relation to every other item, and is perceived from the view-point of the subject as a whole. There are no loose ends in his thoughts, they have been closely knit together in a definite pattern. Most people who complain of bad memories really need discipline in attention, and practice in association. This is especially true of the scattered type of young person who says that he or she has a shockingly bad memory for facts, or for figures, or for faces, or for whatever it may be.

Forgetting, in its way, is as important as remembering. There is an art in forgetting. By thinking a great deal about unimportant trifles they are remembered with an accuracy worthy of matters of greater moment. We have all of us come across the man who can tell you any cricket score since the days of W. G. Grace, or the names of all the winners of all the classical horse races. Other matters which may or may not be more important have got pushed into the hinterland of his mind, and he assures you that he simply cannot remember them.

However, when all due allowance is made for

emotional complexes and inhibitions, memory remains primarily a matter of mind-training ; not by any mechanical process of repetition, but by observing and thinking, by noting and arranging the contents of one's mind as carefully as one notes and arranges the furniture in one's room.

II

There is something sinister as well as subtle about the word suggestion. It calls up visions of villains in the realm of romance who with flashing eyes dominated their victims to the brink of ruin ; yes, and well over the brink, had it not been for handsome heroes with iron wills who knew just how to shatter the hypnotic influence at the crucial moment.

Svengali, it will be remembered, dominated Trilby, hypnotised her, and kept her under the spell of his evil suggestion. Literature of this kind is responsible for the common notion that some people have a power of hypnotism, a faculty of suggestion, which is denied to others. This is not so. Fundamentally there is only one kind of suggestion, the suggestion which one gives to oneself, namely, auto-suggestion. Hetero-suggestion, the suggestion given by somebody else, is a misnomer. There is really no such thing. Other people may present you with ideas, but until you yourself adopt them and give them to yourself, they are of no effect.

But what do we mean by suggestion ? I think it is best defined as ' the subconscious realisation of an idea.' For instance, we may take the case of the bad boy who stood sucking a lemon in front of a street-musician while the latter played a cornet. Very soon the musician conceived the idea of sucking a lemon ; formed a fantasy of the act, and subconsciously realised the idea, with the result that his mouth filled with saliva, and he had to desist from discoursing sweet music.

It is important to notice that the realisation of the idea is subconscious, that is to say, the idea works itself out without any conscious attention being given to it.   A medical friend of mine told me recently of a distinguished colleague of his who was an expert in treating cancer of the breast.   This disease is normally confined to women, yet, through the expert's constant study of the disease and the workings of his imagination, he suggested to himself that he had the disease, whereupon he developed it and recently died of it.

A story is told of a guest in a crowded hotel who had to make the best of poor accommodation. After trying vainly to open a window in his small room, he retired to bed feeling sure that he could not sleep well in such a stuffy atmosphere.   After an hour or so of dozing, he woke up gasping for air.   He got out of bed and groped in the dark for the windowpane.   When at last he knew that his hand was on glass he shattered it with his fist, and then inhaled a deep refreshing draught through the aperture which he had made.   Thoroughly invigorated, he returned to bed to sleep dreamlessly, and to discover next morning that it was the face of a clock and not the window which he had smashed.

How does suggestion work ?   As far back as the third century Tertullian makes a shrewd guess.   He says Nature herself suggests immortality by a certain ' public sense ' with which God has enriched the human soul. By public sense he means a common or general sense as opposed to any particular or individual sense ; a sort of sentient repository of past experience. According to Tertullian it is from this source, this animated reservoir of ideas, that Nature teaches us by suggestion.

By modern psychologists man, in his mental life, has been likened to an iceberg, only one-eighth of which is visible, seven-eighths remaining submerged beneath the surface of the water. The one-eighth which is visible corresponds with consciousness, the seven-eighths with the unconscious.

Now it is contended that everything that ever entered consciousness remains, if not in consciousness, at least in the unconscious. An impression may be buried deep down in the unconscious, but there it is and there it stays, requiring only that you touch the right spring to bring it to the surface.

It is contended that the unconscious in the course of years has co-ordinated all your past experiences, from which it is clear that the unconscious knows more about you than does the conscious. It understands thoroughly your mental, moral, and physical make-up. Is it possible to use this intimate comprehensive knowledge ? It is possible if we escape from the bustle of consciousness, and passively allow the unconscious to motivate and act in tranquillity.

It is sometimes stated that by suggestion it is possible to make a good man perform evil deeds ; in fact, this used to be a favourite theme with novelists.

But personally I do not think so. Even though the hypnotised patient is in a passive and receptive state, he will not accept suggestions which run counter to the whole trend of his unconsciousness. Such a suggestion would not work, for the simple reason that the essence of suggestion is to let the unconscious work in its own consistent way.

Some people are naturally more receptive and suggestive than others, but receptivity can be cultivated in every one by attending to the elementary laws of suggestion. These laws may be reduced to three.

(i) There is first of all the law of concentrated attention. It is necessary at the outset to avoid all distractions and to check all wandering thoughts. To attend to the positive idea of whatever is desired, say physical fitness, to the exclusion of all other ideas. The idea suggested must be positive and in itself attractive. A negative idea, e.g., that you are not ill, is too vague, and if it contradicts experience it cannot possibly be accepted by the unconscious.

The suggestion that you are going to be particularly clear-headed to-day is more likely to be effective. Here there is only one idea at work, one idea to be borne in mind, one idea to realise itself. The suggestion that you are *not* going to be muddle-headed contains two contrary ideas, that of being clear-headed, and that of being muddle-headed. The one counteracts the other, and nothing happens.

(ii) This leads us to consider the law of reversed effort. There are occasions when the more one tries to avoid something, the more one is fascinated by that object and attracted towards it. The more you try to go to sleep the more wakeful you become. A man learning to drive a motor-car tries to avoid a great hole in the middle of the road. The more he tries to avoid it, the more he is drawn to it until finally he is in it. Hence it is important to keep the will out of suggestion. Conation of any kind hinders the working of suggestion. The old advice to make one's mind a perfect blank is good if it could only be executed. It is more practical to attempt suggestion either last thing at night, just before the hypnoidal images grow very clear as you lose consciousness, or first thing in the morning when the mind is empty of cares. Relaxation of all mental effort is essential.

(iii) A third law of considerable consequence is the law of auxiliary emotion. This means that if a suggestion is backed by emotion, that suggestion is more likely to be operative. The suggestion of coming to grief in an examination is heightened by the fear of failure. The incentive to work is greater if there is the added motive of love of one's work. Most men are the architects of their own misfortunes because of the defeatist attitude in which they work. To want to make money and yet always expect to be poor ; to desire success and yet doubt your own abilities, this, says an American writer, is like trying to reach east by travelling west. Fear of failure can paralyse any suggestion. Confidence is great gain, but it must be well founded in truth.

Some years ago I conducted a number of interesting experiments in the matter of measuring suggestibility. A portable box was fitted up elaborately with machinery which produced an easily graduated hum. It was furnished with two handles attached to the box by insulated wires. The schoolchildren who were the subjects of the experiment were asked to hold the handles until they felt that the current was too strong, and then to let go at once. Needless to say, there was no current, but the increasing noise of the machinery as the operator visibly moved the lever supplied all that was required in the way of suggestion.

On the whole the girls were more suggestible than the boys. Out of some four hundred subjects only one, a boy, held on to the bitter end and truthfully maintained that he felt nothing. But, alas, he is a dull boy, bereft of all imagination, unresponsive to the influences of environment and education. For it must not be forgotten that suggestion is a prime factor in the teacher's art.

III

Are we sorry because we cry ? Or do we cry because we are sorry ?

The idea that our emotions, and especially what are called the tender emotions, are merely the automatic consequences of certain physical actions will come as a surprise to many people.

Yet this was the theory put forward in all seriousness by the distinguished American psychologist, William James, and still held by many of his followers. He says : ' The more rational statement is that we feel sorry because we cry, angry because we strike, afraid because we tremble, and not that we cry, strike, or tremble because we are sorry, angry or fearful, as the case may be.'

His view is that the perception of an idea (say, of cold) gives rise to an organic movement (shivering), which is followed by a feeling (of chill). In other words, the symptoms induce the feeling.

In support of the theory it is urged that if you repress the symptoms the feeling will disappear. ' Refuse to express a passion and it dies.' Eliminate all the motions of anger and you cease to be angry ; hence the old advice to count ten before giving vent to your wrath. By the time you have counted ten all feeling of the ire has vanished.

On the other hand, stimulate the symptoms and you increase the feeling. We all know what is meant by working oneself into a passion. Raise the voice, strike the table, and we soon become victims of overpowering emotion.

On a frosty day if you persist in shivering, blowing on your hands, and stamping your feet, you will feel the cold more acutely than if you did not indulge in these symptomatic actions.

Now there is an influential school of psychologists, headed by McDougall, who regard all emotions as being merely the affective sides of instincts. With this school instincts are the hub of the human mechanism ; they are described as the prime movers of all human activity, and the central mystery of life and mind and will. McDougall defines instinct as an innate psychological disposition which *determines* its possessor to do this, that, or the other.

There is no freedom. Instinct rules by hereditary right, and civilised man is sent back to the jungle.

All the noblest human emotions are held to be merely biological products of certain physical tendencies.

Of late years this instinct school has received some support from the psycho-analysts. Thus Oscar Pfister declares that the object of psycho-analysis is to investigate the instinctive forces lying below the threshold of consciousness.

What are these instinctive forces ? They are generally held to be two, namely, the instinct of self-preservation and the instinct of self-reproduction. A little reflection makes it clear that these two instincts are very closely connected, and that they are, in fact, different aspects of the fundamental instinct of vital continuity, which, I imagine, is very much what Bergson means by his *élan vital*.

There are many different groups of materialist psychologists who lay it down that the only function of emotion is to reinforce the instinctive act in the biological interests of the individual or the species.

Some of them, following Herbert Spencer, go to the length of regarding the symptoms of emotions as survivals from actions which were really useful in the barbaric past. The signs of anger in particular, we are told, had their origin in big fights before the Queensberry rules were in force.

Thus the closing of one's eyes in blind rage is regarded as a relic of a necessary protective measure for one's eyesight during a friendly scrap with a neighbour. The angry snort is reminiscent of short-ness of breath in the actual fight, while the dilated nostrils of the infuriated man indicate just how your primitive ancestor managed to breathe when

o

his ' mouth was filled up by a part of an antagonist's body that had been seized.'

At least that is the genesis of emotional gesture according to the gentle Herbert Spencer.

Now ; there are many things to be urged against this crude view of emotion. First of all, emotion is not merely the effective element of instinct ; it is something broader, deeper, and higher than instinct. The term emotion in psychological usage is applied to any marked psychological effect arising in certain complex situations, and the materialists forget that in addition to the crude animal emotions there are emotions attaching to intellectual activity, such as the feelings of wonder and surprise ; to æsthetic feelings, such as the sentiments awakened by the contemplation of the beautiful and the sublime ; and finally to the moral sentiments of responsibility, approbation, disapproval, guilt, remorse.

Is it conceivable that these fine feelings are all intimately bound up with biological instinct ?

Instinct is a tendency to feel in the presence of certain objects. But they are not necessarily the same objects, or the same class of objects, in both cases. In the presence of a mad bull there is a tendency to feel afraid (emotion), and to run away (instinct) ; but in the presence of a beautiful landscape there is the æsthetic tendency to admiration (emotion) whilst there is absolutely no instinct at work, and consequently no reinforcement of an instinctive act.

At best the reinforcement of action can be taken as the aim of only strictly biological emotions such as are found in the brute beasts. In man there is an entirely new factor, reason, which is capable of controlling both instinct and emotion.

That the higher emotions are not linked up with the lower instincts in such a way as to be products of them was recognised long ago by Huxley. He says somewhere : ' Ethical nature, if born of cosmic nature, is certainly at enmity with its parent,' since the ethical emotions do not make for the preservation of the individual or of the species. They have not infrequently led to the martyr's stake and the patriot's grave.

That the symptom is not the cause of the emotion is clear in the case of the higher emotions peculiar to man. A little introspection makes it obvious that in the case of these emotions the symptoms do not precede, but actually follow, a thought-process.

For instance, a man sitting at a card-table hears the word ' cheat ' pronounced, and he remains quite unaffected until he intellectually realises that the taunt is applied to him ; then follow the symptoms of indignation. Clearly in this intellectual emotion it is the feeling that has caused the symptoms, and not vice versa.

A similar thought-process intervenes in the workings of all the higher emotions, in our reactions to a picture, a poem, a symphony, or a moral ideal. Obviously the feelings aroused in these cases are not linked up with any instinct, and consequently instinct cannot be the sole driving force of human life.

It must be remembered that in man instinct dwells side by side with reason. Intelligence does not do away with instinct. The latter has its own proper field of activity, and it seems to me that it finds its legitimate outlet more especially in outdoor games. These games call forth the sterling qualities of mind and body which were required in primitive battles ; courage, endurance, strength, speed, and a sense of solidarity with one's side.

In these primordial strifes of uncivilised men the biological instincts were very active, as indeed they are to-day in such hefty games as Rugger and Soccer. It has often seemed to me that the best footballer is the man who is guided by his instincts ; he does not pause to think, he acts with the sure spontaneity of natural impulse and soon dominates the field.

On the other hand, the brainy player who stops to think, to rationalise his action, is out of his element and usually gets hurt through hesitancy. This is more noticeable perhaps in American football, where the players are clad in armour, and the conditions of primitive warfare are more faithfully ' featured ' than in England. Every now and again one sees a player with the unerring instinct of a Red Indian.

We have had instinct-psychology, psychology without a soul, and the emotional urges of the psycho-analysts, but when all is said and done a sane psychology must recognise the primacy of reason in man. To suppose that he is at the mercy of blind instincts, chemical changes, or burning passions is to overlook the obvious :

> ' Within the brain's most secret cells
> A certain Lord Chief Justice dwells
> Of sovereign power, whom one and all,
> With common voice, we Reason call.'

IV

We have seen that instinct is an inherited tendency to act, and that emotion is an inherited tendency to feel. Habit, on the contrary, is not a legacy either from the race or from our individual ancestors ; it is something which we ourselves acquire, so that our habits may be said to be our very own in a sense which cannot be applied to our instincts and emotions.

We may define habit quite simply as ' an acquired aptitude for some particular mode of action.' Sometimes the aptitude is psychic, of the mental order, as, for instance, when the celebrated judge, Lord Tenterden, expired saying, ' Gentlemen of the Jury, you will now consider your verdict ' ; and sometimes the acquired aptitude is physical, of the bodily order, as for instance, the nervous habit of washing one's hands with invisible soap. However, whether the acquired aptitudes are in the mind or in the body, they are each of them grounded in the organic structure of the creature, and are the outcome of an oft-repeated act. Sense impressions are received and carried along the different nerves to the brain on which they record their report. The rut in the brain grows deeper with each repetition, and both retention and recollection become easier. In fact, Thurot calls habit ' the memory of the organs.'

How far is habit opposed to freedom ? Aristotle answers that though our actions are voluntary throughout, habits are voluntary only as to their beginnings. He points out that when we throw a stone we cannot restrain its flight ; but that, nevertheless, it depended entirely on ourselves whether we should throw it or not. We have all of us seen men become slaves to habit, to the cigarette habit or the pipe habit, or (Heaven forfend this country !) the chewing-gum habit.

Such habits are easily contracted because the actions which build up the habit are pleasurable in themselves, and are calculated to soothe one's agitated feelings and generally steady the nerves. But soon the physical organism craves for the stimulation, and I imagine that most smokers would find it very difficult to give up smoking. I did it myself once for the whole of Lent, and at the end of that period I found, to my astonishment, that I had no inclination to smoke, and, what is more, I have never touched a pipe since in all the seven years that have elapsed.

It may be true that habit is crystallised freedom, but whatever freedom there may be in an ingrained habit it is certainly crystallised, and it is well worth our while to control the crystallisation. As Johnson has it, ' the chains of habit are generally too small to be felt till they are too strong to be broken.'

Habit is like the small stream which, when followed up, carried away the camel with its load. It can change from a useful servant to a tyrannical master. There is something particularly fascinating about mental habits. One comes across a very intelligent man whose wit and wisdom make his conversation a delight, only to learn later that he is a member of some society or organisation which we regard as particularly foolish or obscurantist. Or

we discover that this intelligent gentleman is a
fanatic about something or other that seems to us
utterly unreasonable. Probably he has not been
able to conquer an early acquired habit of mind.
Undoubtedly habit plays a great part in our intellectual make-up, and especially in the mental
moulding of our youth.

Cannibalism appears a thoroughly sound piece of
ethics to the savage who from his tenderest years
has been brought up according to its practical
principles. We all of us take a great deal for
granted in our childhood, and we are naturally dis-
inclined to scrutinise the sayings of our acknowledged guides, but I am not prepared to go as far as
Burke, who declares that, if an idiot were to tell you
the same story every day for a year, you would end
by believing him.

Ethical teachers from Socrates onwards have
realised the importance of forming good habits in
childhood. It is generally held that up to twenty
years of age is the period for the formation of what
are called personal habits, such as diction, accent,
pronunciation, manners, poise of body, and the like,
and it is contended that very rarely does anyone
really learn a foreign language after his twentieth
year. It is still more difficult to unlearn, to undo
early habits.

How few men in later life succeed in eradicating,
say, a cockney accent or a nasal twang contracted
in their youth. The difficulty of learning to dress
properly has proved too much for many a man, and
not a few women, who have made money. The
bounder never succeeds in becoming a gentleman,

not merely because he tries too hard, but chiefly because he simply cannot unravel the past and readapt both his mind and body to a new environment. Alas, you cannot teach an old dog new tricks.

The vital years from the point of view of the formation of vocational and professional habits are held to be those between twenty and thirty. It is then that a man acquires the stamp of his profession or trade. It is curious how a man's vocation marks him, even though he be a misfit. The years of study, apprenticeship, and practice which he has lived have imperceptibly moulded the whole man, rendering disguise impossible for long.

In nature everything tends to a state of fixity ; the bent trees show the direction of the prevailing wind, and the rivulet takes up a definite course on its way to the ocean.

Many years ago the English philosopher Bain formulated two axioms in connection with the fixation of desirable habits which are universally recognised as basic :

(1) Begin with as vigorous and decided an initiative as possible. Fortify yourself at the outset, for instance, by the pressure of public opinion, letting it be known that you are cultivating this or that habit. Do everything you can to reinforce your resolution. You cannot afford to lose a battle in the beginning of this campaign.

(2) Permit no exception until the new habit is rooted. With each exception we slip downhill and have to recover lost ground before we can go on. It is well to remember that in this matter we go

downhill in the fullness of our vigour, and we come back in the extremity of our exhaustion.

To these axioms William James, the American psychologist, has added others of great value.

(1) Make your nervous system your ally instead of your enemy. Do not accustom the organism to strong drink, or to excesses or perversions of any kind. If you do, later on the organism will crave for these things and become your enemy both in the moral and physical sphere. Restraint, temperance, discipline in one's early years result in a lessening of the strife of the members against the mind.

(2) Seize the first opportunity to act on every resolution you make. To put off action is to become a dreamer and a vapid sentimentalist. Don't make the mistakes of thinking you can carry out your resolution whenever you want to : in a crisis you may discover to your sorrow that you cannot do so. To be continually putting off action is to weaken your will-power.

(3) Keep the faculty of effort alive in you by a little gratuitous exercise every day. If an athlete does not exercise he is likely to become muscle-bound and to fail at the big event. The man who can withstand a moral crisis is the man who has deliberately disciplined his mind and temper. Self-control is not something which can be assumed at a moment's notice. It is a habit of mind formed only by laborious and constant practice.

Life has been described as a tissue of habits, and therefore it is essential that from the outset we should carefully watch over their formation. The

Duke of Wellington was wont to say that habit is ten times nature, for it gains strength with each repetition of the act till it ultimately dominates for good or for evil.

v

During the first half of the nineteenth century pessimism as a philosophy of life was exceedingly popular. It owed its vogue to the writings of Schopenhauer, von Hartmann, and Mailaender, and to the plaintive poetry of Heine, Leopardi, and Byron.

The theory was that this is the worst of all possible worlds, and that pain and sorrow and all manner of evil will disappear only when this planet exhibits as few phenomena of life as the moon, or as Swinburne has it, when ' this old earth will be a slag and a cinder wandering round the sun without its crew of fools.'

A first requisite of the pessimistic philosophy was to show that there is more of evil than of good, more of pain than of pleasure in the life of the average man. Some of the attempts made at constructing what has been called a Hedonistic Calculus, a measure of one's pleasurable and painful sensations, are not a little diverting. One disciple of Schopenhauer, a gentleman named Kovalevsky, undertook to keep a diary of his sensations over a period of many months. This he did, but to his chagrin, when he came to formulate his results he found that his painful sensations were quite counterbalanced by his pleasurable ones.

We all know how one great joy can obliterate a

host of minor troubles, and most of us would agree with Herrick that ' there is an hour when one is happy for all one's life,' an hour of rosy optimism when all seems well with the world.

And there are other difficulties about counting your blessings against your troubles. In the Hedonistic Calculus are we to mix up indiscriminately physical and psychic joys ? How can such essentially different qualities be compared ? Am I to set off the intellectual pleasure of solving a problem in trigonometry against the bodily discomfort of a bad soaking in the rain ? Does a half-day's holiday atone for a toothache ? Obviously here the personal equation enters in.

I doubt if it is possible psychologically to establish a purely personal scale for oneself. We are creatures of moods, and the moods are rarely the same for two days in succession. Am I to balance my past pleasures against my present pains ? That does not give me any index as to how happy I am *now*, though I may derive pleasure from reflecting on former happiness, as Virgil counsels us. There are undoubtedly some abiding joys, as there are abiding sorrows. How precisely are they to be estimated ? On the whole, the attempt to prove that the pains of life outweigh its pleasures has not been a success.

Psychologically, sensation is a most elusive process. We use the word to express that change in the state of mind which is produced by an impression upon an organ of sense. It refers explicitly to the modification of our own being, and not to the external objects which give rise to the modification.

Knowledge of these external objects is called perception. By sensation, then, we mean the immediate effects upon consciousness of the nerve-currents to the brain.

Now it has been ascertained by experiment that there is a mathematically definite relation between the external stimulus and the internal sensation.

Let us take as the stimulus a single candle burning faintly. Until the light attains to a certain intensity it does not cause any sensation at all. There is, as it were, a threshold over which the stimulus must pass in order to give rise to sensation. If to a single burning candle another be added we register the increased sensation of light at once. But if a single lighted candle be added to ten burning candles, we experience no increase of sensation. Three extra candles would need to be added for us to perceive any increase in illumination ; and if a hundred candles were lit, thirty more would need to be added before we experienced an increased sensation of light.

So, too, is it with sound and pressure. If three voices are singing and another joins in, we notice the increased volume of sound at once. But if ten are singing, three voices would have to be added before we should detect any difference, and in the case of a mighty choir of one hundred voices it would be necessary to add at least thirty to gain an appreciable effect.

Weber first noticed the operation of this law in connection with weights. He found as a result of a number of experiments that, no matter what weight you started with, the fraction to be added in order to gain an increase in sensation was always about one-third of the original stimulus. Technically, the law states that the sensation increases as the logarithm of the stimulus ; in other words, that the stimulus must increase in geometric progression (1, 2, 4, 8) in order to increase the intensity of sensation in arithmetic progression (1, 2, 3, 4).

The law holds, at least approximately, in the sphere of physical sensation. It is an easy matter to test it and verify it for oneself. Furthermore, it works roughly with regard to the psychic faculty of judgment in relation to the measurement of space and time. Thus, in order to judge a line to be twice as long as another, it has to be more than twice as long, and the distinguished psychologist, Mark Baldwin, has discovered that in estimating five seconds you will make the time too short by about one-fourth.

You can make the experiment by counting the seconds first with your eyes on the second hand of a watch, and then with your eyes closed. But can the law be extended to the strictly psychic sphere ? Is it necessary, for instance, that the stimulus of happiness shall be multiplied by three before we are appreciably any happier than we were ? Professor Münsterberg contended that this is so, and he used the Weber-Fechner Law as the basis of a psychological argument against Socialism. He argues that the simple pleasures of life which satisfy a man who is earning, say, £2 a week, will fail to stimulate the same man when he gets £5 a week. He will then want more than three times the means of enjoyment which he had formerly.

And so it will go on, every increase in salary automatically raising the standard necessary for happiness. Münsterberg is not arguing against Socialism as an economic or political system ; he is merely contending that £1 a day for life for every man would not make people, on the whole, any happier than they are at present.

The same argument has been advanced with condemnation of the modern method of bringing up children in a certain section of society. Every conceivable pleasure is given to the child. He is loaded with playthings and presented with magnificent mechanical toys beyond his understanding. He is taken to cinemas, plays and parties, with the result that he is completely *blasé* at eleven years of age.

Civilised man has created many wants for himself, and he goes on creating them, all unconscious of the working of the psychological law as to the relativity of pleasure to its causes.

One of the commonest errors is that new sensations mean happiness. This is very far from being the case.

I have met American tourists amid classical ruins in Italy experiencing new sensations, but I am sure that these good people would have been far happier in a cinema. The sensations which they were actually experiencing were not at all what they had expected to experience. They had not the necessary cultural background to experience any sensation other than that of surprise tinged with disappointment. The ways of the ancient Romans did not appeal to them.

It is well to remember that too much stimulation causes pain. A blinding light flashed into one's eyes, a loud banging close to one's ears, exposure to a scorching sun or an arctic frost, all these can inflict both agony and injury.

And so, too, is it in the higher sphere ; in the things of the spirit, let stimulation be moderate that happiness may abound.

VI

Does the rising generation read Stevenson, or is he more or less abandoned, like Dickens and Scott ?

Are the youth of to-day first horrified at the deeds of Mr. Hyde and then amazed to discover that that monster was none other than the benevolent Dr. Jekyll himself ? Do they go on to discuss whether Dr. Jekyll and Mr. Hyde were really two distinct personalities or merely alternating presentations of one complex consciousness ?

Stevenson's story is so weird we feel that it cannot be true, and yet truth is oftentimes stranger than fiction, and the sober annals of experimental psychology record some very remarkable cases of what appear to be multiple personality.

Broadly we may divide these cases into two classes :

(1) Cases of successive manifestation of radically altered mentality, and

(2) Cases of simultaneous manifestations of dual consciousness.

(1) In the first class there is the case of Felida, of Bordeaux. At the age of fifteen she fell into a

swoon lasting only a few minutes, and came out of it apparently a totally different person. In her normal state (No. 1) she was serious, morose, obstinate, of mediocre ability, and very industrious. In her secondary state (No. 2) she was gay, boisterous, pliant, decidedly clever, and very idle.

She alternated from state No. 1 to state No. 2 for more than thirty years. We are told that in state No. 1 there was complete forgetfulness of state No. 2. She was ignorant, for instance, of the death of her sister-in-law, which occurred while she was in state No. 2. Similar cases have been presented by Dr. Morton Prince and by Professor Jung in his *Analytical Psychology* under the heading ' Changes in Character and Somnambulistic Personalities,' while Janet records a case of three alternating personalities in an ordinary French peasant woman.

How are we to explain these phenomena ?

The generally accepted definition of person is that of Boethius : ' An individual substance of a rational nature.' Now in these interesting cases of alternating mental states is the unity of psychic life ruptured in such a way that we get two individual substances, that is to say, two separate mental existences ?

I would answer unhesitatingly that the unity of consciousness remains unimpaired, that whatever ' disruption ' there may be is superficial and more apparent than real. Cases of so-called alternating personality are very rare, and, unfortunately, it must be admitted that even in scientific reports on these cases there are exaggerations and unconscious misstatements.

We are told, for instance, that Felida No. 1 could

not remember anything about Felida No. 2.   An inquiry made it abundantly clear that Felida No. 1 and Felida No. 2 had a mass of common experience. Thus they spoke the same language, and knew the same persons, places, and things.   More careful observation tended to show that these diverse personalities merged in a fundamental identity of consciousness.

We must carefully distinguish between the Pure Ego of the German metaphysicians and the Empirical Self of modern psychologists.   By the Pure Ego is meant the I that knows ; by the Empirical Me, the I that is known.

' Know thyself ' was the maxim of one of the world's greatest thinkers, Socrates, and certainly no advice is more difficult to translate into action. Oliver Wendell Holmes says that when two people meet there are really six present, because each person represents three selves.   There is in me (a) the I that I think I am, and this picture in most cases is apt to be somewhat flattering ; (b) the I that others think I am, and this picture is not quite so flattering, as we are reminded by Burns' disquieting lines :

> Oh, wad some power the giftie gie us
> To see oursel's as others see us.

(c) And finally there is the I that I am, the great enigma.   It is in the search for the solution of the great enigma that modifications of consciousness take place which seem to result in new personalities. William James has pointed out that the Empirical Me presents many different social sides to different social groups.

P

A policeman may be stern with a thief and tender with his children. An employer may be strict with his employees but a most indulgent husband.

But in these cases there is no difficulty in harmonising the sternness with the tenderness and the strictness with the indulgence, but there are other cases where a real reconciliation cannot be effected, as, for instance, when a young man gets into bad company and adopts the code of his fellows, meantime trying to present a totally different standard of ethics to his family and to respectable people in general. He is heading rapidly for a disruption in the social self, the kind of thing which is usually preceded by a nervous breakdown.

The influence of mind in moulding so-called secondary personalities is very great, and is seen among mentally deranged people, who very often are sane enough on every question other than that of their personal identity.

In fact, when we come to consider the matter we cannot but marvel how easily changes of character in the broad sense are brought about.

Thus a letter containing bad news will alter a man's tone for the whole day, whereas a hot meal at the right psychological moment will transform a coward into a hero.

With regard to simultaneous manifestations of dual consciousness the difficulty is not so great. Jules Verne is said to have dictated four letters while he wrote a fifth, and similar stories are told of Napoleon and others. It is in reality a question of how many operations the mind can attend to at one and the same time.   If the operations are different we may attend to a number.

Thus it is possible to work a sum in multiplication and recite a verse of poetry simultaneously without any loss of time.   But it would be by no means so easy to write down one verse of poetry while reciting another.   Still, with practice, such things can be done, but obviously the best of these cases does not constitute anything approaching simultaneous dual personality.   They are merely clever tricks of divided attention.

THE QUESTION OF REUNION

(A Paper Read to the [Anglican] Society of St. Thomas of Canterbury, July, 1922)

NOWADAYS one can hardly pick up a serious monthly review, or any of the more expensive weeklies, without coming across an article, sometimes more than one article, bearing on the problem of Christian reunion. Even the illustrated Sunday papers take an interest in the matter, and from time to time provide their readers with solutions to the problem, furnished by people who are held to be mouthpieces of public opinion. The general impression is that all this seeking and striving after unity in religious matters is something begotten of the World War, part of the general reaction away from strife and discussion in favour of universal peace. The Bishops of Peterborough, Zanzibar, and Hereford, whilst rejecting the ' very common assertion that this change [from the stage of pious aspirations to that of practical politics] is due mainly to the war,'[1] nevertheless assign a very recent origin to the movement towards reunion. In their opinion ' the year 1910 will possibly come to be regarded by the historians of the future as the *annus mirabilis* of the movement,' because of the Missionary Conference

---

[1] *Lambeth and Reunion*, pp. 26, 27.

at Edinburgh which imparted to the movement an
impetus from abroad, and also because of the
Resolution of the General Convention of the Protestant Episcopal Church, held at Cincinnati, Ohio,
in the United States of America, in October of the
same year, which provided for the establishment of
a Joint Commission to arrange for a World Conference on Faith and Order. Again, the first of the
' Documents bearing on the Problem of Christian
Unity and Fellowship,'[1] gathered together for the
convenience of those considering the subject of
Christian reunion at the time of the recent Lambeth
Conference, dates back no further than 1916.

In all this there is a tendency to ignore the past
and to treat reunion as though it were a new, instead
of an old problem. As a matter of fact, the Reformation had hardly set in before its chief architects, the
very pioneers of disruption, assumed the rôle of
champions of religious unity. Cranmer's ideal of a
' true Catholicism throughout all Europe ' differs
little, if at all, from the ' ideal of a united and truly
Catholic Church ' commended in their Encyclical
Letter by the Bishops recently assembled at Lambeth
as affording ' a new approach to reunion.'[2] Ever
since Cranmer's day principles of disruption and
aspirations for unity have gone hand in hand in this
country, possibly because, as Mr. Belloc somewhere
suggests, the English people lost the tradition of
clear thinking at the Reformation. However that
may be, in the centuries that have elapsed there have
been innumerable theories of reunion put forward by

---

[1] Published by the S.P.C.K., 1920.
[2] *Conference of Bishops of the Anglican Communion*, p. 12.

men of good will who have striven to effect some kind of compromise between Catholic and Protestant principles.

These various efforts, it seems to me, may be classified roughly under three broad headings :

(1) There is, first of all, the appeal to the undivided church of antiquity.

(2) There is, secondly, the appeal to what may be described as the ' least common denominator ' of Christian belief at the present moment.

(3) There is, finally, the appeal to the living consciousness of Christendom and to inner experience.

I propose briefly to examine these three theories before approaching the problem from the Catholic standpoint.

(1) The appeal to the undivided church of antiquity.[1] As an advocate of this method of approach to the problem of reunion we cannot select anyone more thoroughly representative than Bishop Gore, who, in his *Basis of Anglican Fellowship* (p. 50) says :

' To accept the Anglican position as valid, in any sense, is to appeal behind the Pope and the authority of the medieval church which developed the Papacy

---

[1] In fairness to the propounders of this theory I adopt their phraseology whilst protesting against its implications. The expression ' the undivided church of antiquity ' implies that there is no undivided church of to-day, and lends colour to the concept of a number of partial expressions of the Christian ideal as legitimately constituting, in their totality, a divided church of Christ. Such a concept obscures the real effect of heresy and schism, which is not to divide the church, but to divide sectaries from the church. In Catholic doctrine there is no place for the concept of a divided church. Unity is an essential mark of the Church of Christ which consequently always was, is, and will be undivided.

to the undivided church, and with the undivided church to Scripture as limiting for ever the articles of faith to the original creed.'

His Lordship, it will be noticed, appeals to ' the undivided church ' as one appeals to the Roman Empire, or the French Revolution, or any other un-doubted historical fact, the general character of which is well known. In this way he perpetrates a logical theft which is detected when we ask the vital questions : what was this undivided church ? when did it exist ? and when did it cease to exist ? Here, at the outset, in answer to the question, what was the undivided church of antiquity ? it will be well to clear away a common misconception. It is as-sumed by many that there was a time when all who professed themselves Christians did actually keep the unity of the spirit in the bond of peace. As a matter of historical fact there never was such a time. Even in St. Paul's day there were incipient sects amongst the Corinthians, to whom he found it necessary to address the startling question, ' Is Christ divided ? ' (1 Cor. i, 12, 13). And St. Peter, referring probably to the Nicholaites and Simonites, warns the faithful against ' lying teachers who shall bring in sects of perdition ' (2 Peter ii, 1). In its infancy the Church was distracted by the weird and wild speculations of Ebionites, Gnostics, and Encra-tites. A complete list of the heretics and schismatics who cut themselves off from the Church of Christ prior to the First General Council of Nicæa would be a lengthy one. To mention only a few of the more notorious, there was Saturninus who perverted the Scriptures with his innumerable commentaries, and

Basilides who denied the humanity of Christ. Before the middle of the second century Valentinus from Egypt and Cerdo from Syria were propagating their errors in Rome itself. A little later came Apelles, Potitus, Basiliscus, and Synaros, each with no mean following. There were, too, Adoptionists and Monarchians, and later Sabellians with their errors on the doctrine of the Trinity, and Montanists with their rigorous views on the remission of sin. There were Marcionites, Novatians, and some seventy different sects of Manichæans—all striving to rend the seamless robe of Christ, even before the First Œcumenical Council.

The appeal, then, is not being made to an undivided church in the sense of a church which actually received the allegiance of all who accounted themselves followers of Christ. To what, then, is it being made ? In reality it is being made simply and solely to the early Councils of that great historic Church which, whatever else it did, unhesitatingly denounced and excommunicated heretics throughout the ages. That right is conceded to the church fully and freely in the matter of denouncing heretics who no longer exist—in her condemnation of Gnosticism and Manichæanism she wins the universal applause of Christendom. But as soon as the church touches live issues that self-same right is denied her, and a time-limit is set to her powers. Though the church was from the first invaded by innumerable heresies, apparently she is to be considered immune and intact until a heresy appears which has some affinity with the teaching of one or other modern religious body. Consequently we receive very different answers to the very pertinent question, when did the church cease to be undivided ?

(i) Some, who accept the decrees of the Council of Chalcedon, place the division at the sixth Œcumenical Council in A.D. 681.

(ii) More generally the line is drawn at the Council of Chalcedon itself in A.D. 451.

(iii) Others, with the Nestorians, say the church ceased to be undivided at the Council of Ephesus in A.D. 431.

(iv) Others, again, with the Arians, declare that it ceased to be undivided at the Council of Nicæa, and we have the authority of Dr. Jowett for the statement that a distinguished Anglican prelate once declared that ' the decision of Nicæa was the greatest misfortune that ever befell the Christian world.'[1]

It is impossible, then, to get any general agreement as to when the church was undivided. Even so, we may proceed to ask a further vital question : in what sense do those who appeal to the undivided church accept the decisions of what they regard as the undivided church ? What, for instance, does Bishop Gore mean when he lays it down that ' the dogmatic decisions of the undivided church about the person of Christ have been truly inspired by the Spirit of Truth ? '[2] Does this mean that the decisions are to be accepted as final and binding ? One would have thought so, had not his Lordship proceeded to elucidate his meaning. He is careful to add : ' These decisions are to be regarded as primarily

---

[1] *Essays and Reviews : On the Interpretation of Scripture,* p. 420.

[2] *Bampton Lectures on the Incarnation.*

negative . . . ; they leave us always in the position of men who go back for their positive information about the person of our Lord chiefly to the picture in the Gospels, and the interpretation of the Apostles.' That is to say, his Lordship accepts the decisions of the undivided church as being divinely inspired, but nevertheless holds himself free to interpret them in the light of his own understanding of the Gospels and the teaching of the Apostles. This surely is a curious way of accepting decisions—a subjective method which can lead only to further divisions and subdivisions amongst those who practise it.

It would seem, then, that the appeal to the undivided church of antiquity is not likely to furnish us with a satisfactory basis for reunion, since, in the first place, there is no general agreement as to when the church is supposed to have become divided, and, secondly, because the decrees of even the earliest Councils are accepted with reservations of such a character as to render the acceptance ' not negotiable.'

(2) We may now proceed to consider the appeal to the least common denominator of current Christian belief. This popular idea has many popular exponents who present it in attractive guises. At one time we heard a great deal of the need for a ' common platform,' but following in the wake of the League of Nations came the inevitable proposal for a League of Churches. Thus, Canon Streeter, writing in the *Daily News* a few years ago, said : ' The time is ripe for a League of Churches, and if organised Christianity is to make any contribution to the problems

of our time, it must be formed.'[1] One fancies that
the analogy between politics and religion, which at
first gained favour for the proposal, ultimately gave
it its death-blow. It is impossible to close one's eyes
to the fact that politics, even in the wider sense of
Aristotle, are concerned with establishing relations
which are essentially temporary, and largely, if not
wholly, pragmatic ; whereas religion is, or ought to
be, concerned with the eternal and the true.   The
man-in-the-street feels that in religion, at all events,
it ought not to be a case of ' nothing continueth in
one stay.' There he does expect to get a firm foot-
hold of some kind.   Hence the frank and open
proposal for a round-table conference of churches
committed only to the principle of barter and
exchange has found little or no favour with people
to whom religion is a reality.   The proposal is more
attractive when the principle is somewhat disguised.
The recent Lambeth Conference furnishes a good
instance of this tortuous method of approach. The
pith of the Conference may be stated in the words of
Dr. Headlam : ' The Church of England has definitely
stated that it is prepared not to insist upon any other
formula except the Nicene Creed, it gives up as
necessary either the 39 articles or the Athanasian
Creed.' Here, though a dogmatic stand is taken, the
principle underlying the statement is again that of
barter and exchange.   It is a case of *do ut des*, as
witness the reception of the proposal by a well-
known Congregationalist, who declared, at the
Geneva Conference following the Lambeth Conference, that ' the Church of England has reached

[1] August 27th, 1918.

the last limit of concession which can be expected, and may reasonably ask that other religious bodies should receive their proposals in the same spirit of faith and good will in which these have been made.'[1] But where is the guarantee that the last limit of concession has been reached ? Who is to say that the whittling down process will not continue at future Lambeth Conferences ? The effect of this most recent concession has been stated succinctly by one who is in full sympathy with the proposal and eminently qualified to speak : ' Anglicanism as a model is dead,' declares the Bishop of Zanzibar. And every religious body which enters into the scheme must merge its identity in mutual concession, possibly to the vanishing-point of all Christian belief.

Certainly there is no finality in the particular basis of reunion selected by the Lambeth Conference—the Nicene Creed. It is not, and was never intended to be, an epitome of Christian doctrine. ' Bible Christians ' will point out that the Nicene Creed says never a word with regard to the authority of the Scriptures, or the nature and extent of inspiration ; on the other hand, neither does it exact belief in a divinely appointed episcopate, the priesthood, or the sacramental system. Are all these vital points to be waived simply because they find no place in an ancient creed which was drawn up to meet the needs of an epoch when Christians were united on many of the questions which are most hotly disputed at the present day ? By many it is tacitly assumed that the Nicene Creed is a complete presentation of

[1] *Church Quarterly Review*, October, 1921, p. 154.

Christian belief in the year A.D. 325 ; yet it is difficult
to understand how any serious student of history
can make such an assumption. To the Nicene Creed
in particular we may apply the profound saying of
Abelard with regard to theology in general, that it
owes its development to the challenges of the
heretics, without which it would never have reached
its firmness and precision. No one can doubt that
the Nicene Creed would have been different had the
third and fourth centuries been distinguished by
controversies as to the nature and constitution of
the Church, instead of by Christological controversies. For the simple reason that the Nicene
Creed does not touch many of the most vital issues
of the present day it is useless as a basis of reunion.
Surely there is no religious body laying claim to the
name Christian which does not, in its own sense,
subscribe to the Nicene Creed already. Obviously it
is not the creed, but the interpretations of the creed
which matter, unless agreement between the different
religious bodies is to be merely on paper. Even
taking the Nicene Creed as a basis, we are forced
back upon the necessity of some living voice to
interpret it, and to interpret it in the light
of ever-increasing scientific and philosophical
knowledge.

To the Catholic mind there is a fundamental misconception underlying all such proposals. If, indeed,
Christianity is a divinely revealed religion, as it
professes to be, it follows that Christians are not at
liberty to bargain and barter amongst themselves as
to how much, or how little, of that revelation they
shall accept. Though her position be strictly logical,

the finality of the attitude of the Catholic Church towards revealed truth is, in many quarters, either not sufficiently recognised or sadly misunderstood. Thus, the Bishops of Peterborough, Zanzibar, and Hereford, in their brochure *Lambeth and Reunion,* say :

' With regard to the Roman Church nothing more can be recorded than a change of personal relations. The position is summed up in the words describing the reception by the Pope of the deputation visiting Europe and the East on behalf of the Commission of the World Conference on Faith and Order. The Pope " received us most cordially. He answered most distinctly. The contrast between the Pope's attitude towards us and his official attitude towards the Conference was very sharp. The one was irresistibly benevolent, the other irresistibly rigid " ' (p. 29).

Here, as elsewhere, there is no recognition of the fact that the rigidity is not a matter of choice nor of policy, but, from the standpoint of Catholicism, as much a matter of necessity as the rigid attitude of every sane man towards the multiplication table. As yet, in this country, many zealous workers for re-union have not grasped the fact that the principle of barter and exchange in doctrinal matters, how-ever attractive it may sound to English ears, is positively blasphemous to those who believe that no one has right to tamper with the deposit of revealed truth. We, at least, hear ringing in our ears the charge of St. Paul : ' keep that which is committed to thy trust ' (1 Tim. vi, 20).

(3) There is, in the third place, the appeal to Christian consciousness, to inner experience, and to the subjective values of Christianity.

Those who advocate this method of the inner approach insist that if formulæ unite, they also divide, and that consequently they are better eschewed. Thus, Canon Bindley, at the Modern Churchmen's Congress held at Cambridge in the summer of 1921, said boldly : ' We need to find out, not a formula, but a temper—not a Creed, but a Faith—which is common to all, and which underlies all, and supports all, and inspires all.'[1] We are reminded of Huxley's famous dictum, ' Agnosticism is not a creed, but a method,' and in both cases it is a method which leads inevitably to doubt and disbelief. The aim of reunion, we are told, is to include, not to exclude, and hence, says Canon Bindley : ' We need a confession of faith in which the essentials are implicit, rather than a Creed which attempts to make them explicit.' Definition is to be avoided as trammelling freedom of thought and lowering subjective values.

It is generally recognised that the last twenty years represent something more than the conventional dawn of a new century. Already a new spirit, elusive and perplexing, is discernible in life and literature. It is difficult to describe and impossible to define, but if the thirteenth century stands out as the golden age of metaphysics, and the seventeenth as heralding the reign of the physical sciences, we may perhaps not inaptly describe the present as a psychological age. No longer is psychology ' the

[1] *The Modern Churchman*, September, 1921, p. 310.

Cinderella of the Sciences,' rather is she the Queen of the Muses. There is a psychology not merely of life, but of art, literature, and music—and there is, too, a psychological, or pseudo-psychological, method of approaching all religious problems. As an illustration of it I may perhaps be permitted to cite the following passage from a speaker at the Cambridge Congress :

'Experimental psychology could render most important service to Christian theology if it could show us how to make contact, to use William James's phrase, with the spirit of God. Until we have such knowledge every aspect of the interaction of the human and the divine will be a mystery. I imagine that our ignorance in this region has caused us to avoid questions concerning reconciliation, redemption, salvation. I regret the omission, because such matters are central to Christian experience.'[1]

Apparently we are to despair of acquiring an adequate knowledge of Christian teaching until such time as empiric psychology has attained a much fuller development. Are we to discount the theology of Augustine, Anselm, and Aquinas because they lacked proficiency in experimental psychology ?

But whither is this method of the inner approach leading ? The answer is not far to seek. Apparently every article of the Creed is to be translated into terms of personal consciousness, and accepted only in so far as it finds any warrant in that consciousness. In this way even the Divinity of Christ is rejected, and historic Christianity tumbles to the

[1] *The Modern Churchman*, September, 1921, pp. 346, 347.

ground a mass of ruins. But that is not all. This introspective method, with its semi-deification of human consciousness, has led to a pseudo-mysticism, the direct outcome of which is pantheism. The belief even in a personal God is disappearing at the bidding of this modern appeal to consciousness. Obviously this method of approach to the problem of reunion can lead only to a unity of negation—the negation of every article of the Christian creed.

(4) Is there, then, no hope of Christian reunion ? I am sanguine enough to think that there is, but that it must be sought on different lines.

In the first place, instead of aspiring after an ideal unity, I would ask you to contemplate the very real diversity which exists amongst us. At a very modest estimate we will suppose that there are a hundred different religious bodies in England to-day. If you went back a hundred years, there would hardly be more than fifty. If you went back another hundred years, you would find a proportionate decrease, whilst if you went back to Luther's day, you would find only two—the old historic church and the new comprehensive church which had broken away from it. Now I am going to ask you to go back to the days prior to Martin Luther, when, as a matter of fact, you will find only one historic Church. I ask you to go back to the thirteenth century, and seek there a basis of Christian unity. That basis, it seems to me, you will find in the writings of St. Thomas Aquinas.

To most people he is merely a name, or at best the author of the *Summa*. But the *Summa*, master-piece as it is, is only one portion—less than half—of

Q

his voluminous writings. St. Thomas's intellectual preoccupation was with philosophy, and in meeting the challenges of heretics he is always at pains to refute them from the standpoint of reason. If I were to summarise in a sentence the achievement of Aquinas I would say that he translated into terms of common-sense Realism the doctrines of Christianity as vindicated against heretics in previous centuries. Consequently his works constitute a monumental apologetic setting forth the complete accord between reason and revelation. On this point I will content myself with quoting the remarkable words of a great non-Catholic scholar, Dr. Wicksteed. In his Hibbert Lectures on *The reactions between Dogma and Philosophy illustrated from the works of St. Thomas Aquinas*, he says :

' The conditions under which St. Thomas Aquinas undertook his great synthesis of dogma and philosophy combined with the special characteristics of his genius, constantly invite us to step beyond the limits of his own creed and church ; for his works present us with luminous examples of phenomena common to all advanced religious evolutions. They teach us to recognise the same underlying problems and analogous attempts to solve them, under the widest diversity of technical expression. They perpetually provoke us to deeper and more fearless thought, and they are as rich in impressive and even terrible warnings as they are in guidance and stimulation ' (p. 1).

With regard to the method of St. Thomas Aquinas I may perhaps be permitted to say a word. He clearly defines the boundaries of the provinces of reason and revelation. Thus he writes : ' by natural reason we can know of God only what necessarily belongs to Him as the principle of all things. . . . What is of faith can be proved by authority alone to those who receive the authority ; while as regards others it suffices to prove that what faith teaches is not impossible ' (*Sum. Theol.*, I, *Qu.* 32, *Art.* I). The *Summa* is primarily an exposition of the Christian Faith, that is of Christian principles and their mani-fold application in thought and action. Here the method of St. Thomas is certainly not

> The stern and prompt suppressing
> As an obvious deadly sin
> All the questioning and the guessing
> Of the soul's own soul within :

rather is it the peremptory challenging of every-thing which claims to enter the Temple of Truth. Every conceivable objection—from Scripture, from the Fathers, from pagan philosophers, from pure reason—is urged fully and with perfect frankness against every dogma of revealed religion. And here, naturally, St. Thomas answers the objections from the standpoint of a Christian, with divine revelation as his final court of appeal. But it was necessary for him to adopt a very different standpoint in dealing with the Arabian philosophers. As Mohammedans they refused to admit either the Scriptures or Christian tradition as sources of revealed truth, and consequently in refuting the Arabians St. Thomas was thrown back upon the basis of pure reason. He therefore set himself to review the grounds of theistic belief in the light of the newly recovered speculations of Aristotle. It was in this way that his great philosophical work, the *Contra Gentiles*, came to be written, to establish by the light of reason the truths of the natural law and the moral necessity of revelation. In the combination of the *Contra Gentiles* and the *Summa* we have an unrivalled presentation of natural and revealed religion by one who was at once a great saint and a great scholar, and we ask you to make the acquaintance of these writings for several reasons.

(*a*) First of all, in these writings there can be no bias or prejudice against religious bodies which are the outcome of the Reformation, since St. Thomas wrote centuries before these bodies existed. His writings are high above the storm and stress of the religious controversies that distract this land to-day. I invite you, therefore, to read them and see what Christians really did believe before the disruption of Western Christendom. Surely we can find no better basis for Christian unity than the basis upon which the whole Western Church did actually take its stand. I have often wished that the masses in this country could have the opportunity of reading what St. Thomas Aquinas wrote. The Dominican translation of the *Summa* is beyond the means of the man-in-the-street, and in any case he would not care to tackle such large volumes. One would like to see various points of Catholic teaching translated from St. Thomas and published in pamphlet form, the inside cover of each pamphlet setting forth who Aquinas was, and the all-important fact that he wrote before the disruption of Christendom, and consequently without bias against the modern sects.

Such a plain exposition of what Christians believed before the disruption of the Reformation would surely pave the way to reunion.

(*b*) Again I venture to say that members of every Christian body will find in the *Summa* many of their most cherished beliefs expressed far better than they can express them themselves. I am not alluding merely to the truths of natural religion or to the fact of a revelation, but to what are sometimes erroneously called distinctively Protestant doctrines —such doctrines as the Atonement, the Sacrifice of Calvary, the One Mediatorship of Christ, the workings of the Holy Spirit in the souls of men, and more especially the high authority of scriptural proof.

(*c*) But you will find more than that. You will find that in a great many theological questions you have absolute intellectual liberty. You will learn the vital distinction between the essentials of Christianity and the things that are not essential, and realise the importance of holding fast at all costs to those essentials. You will find in this most wonderful expression of Christian belief something that will make an irresistible appeal to the mind that conceives, and the heart that aspires after, Christian unity : you will find Truth.

Now I would like to put to you the startling question, what is the use of Truth ? There are people in this country who tell you that speculative truth is of no use at all. That cannot be so. If we have got Truth, we have got something that can be translated into life and action, and in that precisely lies its use and its value. A truth of the abstract order, such a truth, for instance, as that any two sides of a triangle are together greater than the third, is translated into action by all of us when we hurry to the railway station to catch a train. So, too, with the truths of the speculative theology of Aquinas. If you tell me that these cannot be translated into action, I point to the humble followers of St. Francis of Assisi who lived them, or to the schools for the education of the masses which grew out of them, and which later developed into the great historic universities of Europe. Or I might point to Giotto and the whole school of Italian painters, or to the sublime Dante who was proud to acknowledge that he derived his inspiration from Aquinas. Or I might ask you to look upon the glorious Gothic cathedrals which embodied the principles of Aquinas in stone, or simply to look back through the noble ruins of the pre-Reformation churches and abbeys of this land, back through their shattered glories, to the living faith of those who built them.

I ask you, then, not to look to the dim distant future, full of uncertainties, with a vague hope that some blind evolution of forces will work out towards that unity which we all so earnestly desire. I bid you rather look back to that golden period of culture, thought, and action, when the social fabric of Europe was based upon the concept of a religious unity than which in the history of Christianity no more perfect has ever been manifest. For the actual expression of that concept I have pointed to the works of that great synthetic genius, St. Thomas of Aquin.

With that so nobly realised ideal before our eyes, we may turn to the future with hope and confidence.

An equally realisable ideal, the edifice of a no less perfect unity, glows before us through the present dimness and the mists. If we are ever to realise it, it will not be by building with loose stones upon an unstable foundation. We must build with the same stones and upon the same foundation with which Aquinas built in the thirteenth century.

THE END